Acoustic and Auditory Phonetics

SECOND EDITION

Acoustic and Auditory Phonetics

KEITH JOHNSON

Blackwell
Publishing

BLACKWELL PUBLISHING
350 Main Street, Malden, MA 02148-5020, USA
9600 Garsington Road, Oxford OX4 2DQ, UK
550 Swanston Street, Carlton, Victoria 3053, Australia

First edition published 1997
Second edition published 2003 by Blackwell Publishing Ltd

6   2006

Library of Congress Cataloging-in-Publication Data

Johnson, Keith, 1958–
Acoustic and auditory phonetics / Keith Johnson.—2nd ed.
p. cm.
Includes bibliographical references and index.
ISBN 1–4051–0122–9 (hb : alk. paper) — ISBN 1–4051–0123–7 (pb : alk. paper)
1. Phonetics, Acoustic. 2. Hearing. I. Title.
P221.5 .J64 2003
414—dc21
2002026253

ISBN-13: 978-1-4051-0122-6 (hb : alk. paper) – ISBN-13: 978-1-4051-0123-3 (pb : alk. paper)

A catalogue record for this title is available from the British Library.

Set in 10 / 12.5pt Palatino
by Graphicraft Ltd, Hong Kong
Printed and bound in Singapore
by C.O.S. Printers Pte Ltd

The publisher's policy is to use permanent paper from mills that operate a sustainable forestry
policy, and which has been manufactured from pulp processed using acid-free and elementary
chlorine-free practices. Furthermore, the publisher ensures that the text paper and cover board
used have met acceptable environmental accreditation standards.

For further information on
Blackwell Publishing, visit our website:
www.blackwellpublishing.com

Contents

Acknowledgments

I started work on this book in 1993 at the Linguistics Institute in Columbus, Ohio, and am grateful to the Linguistic Society of America and particularly the directors of the 1993 Institute (Brian Joseph, Mike Geis, and Lyle Campbell) for giving me the opportunity to teach that summer. I also appreciate the feedback given to me by students in that course and in subsequent phonetics courses that I have taught at Ohio State University.

Peter Ladefoged had much to do with the fact that this book was published (for one thing he introduced me to Philip Carpenter of Blackwell Publishing). I also cherish our conversations about the philosophy of textbook writing and about the relative merits of Anglo-Saxon and Romance words. John Ohala commented extensively on an early draft with characteristic wit and insight, and Janet Pierrehumbert sent me ten long e-mail messages detailing her suggestions for revisions and describing her students' reactions to the manuscript. I appreciate their generosity, and absolve them of responsibility for any remaining errors.

I am very fortunate to work in an incredibly supportive and inspiring environment at Ohio State University. Mary Beckman provided me with encouragement and extensive and very valuable notes on each of the book's chapters. Additionally, Ilse Lehiste, Tsan Huang, Janice Fon, and Matt Makashay gave me comments on the new speech perception chapter, and Beth Hume discussed the perception data in chapters 6–9 with me. Osamu Fujimura discussed the acoustic analysis in chapter 9 with me (he doesn't agree with the presentation there).

My brother, Kent Johnson, produced the best figures in the book (figures 3.1, 3.5a, and 5.7).

For additional comments and suggestions I thank Suzanne Boyce, Ken deJong, Simon Donnelly, Edward Flemming, Sue Guion, Rob Hagiwara, SunAh Jun, Joyce McDonough, Terrence Nearey, Hansang Park, Bob Port (who shared his DSP notes with me), Dan Silverman, and Richard Wright. Thanks also to those who took the time to complete an "adopter survey" for Blackwell. These anonymous comments were very helpful. Many thanks to Tami Kaplan and Sarah Coleman of Blackwell, who helped me complete the second edition.

This book is dedicated to my teachers: Mary Beckman, Rob Fox, Peter Ladefoged, Ilse Lehiste, and David Pisoni.

K. J.

Introduction

This is a short, nontechnical introduction (suitable as a supplement to a general phonetics or speech science text) to four important topics in acoustic phonetics: (1) acoustic properties of major classes of speech sounds, (2) the acoustic theory of speech production, (3) the auditory representation of speech and (4) speech perception. I wrote the book for students in introductory courses in linguistic phonetics, speech and hearing science, and in those branches of electrical engineering and cognitive psychology that deal with speech.

The first five chapters introduce basic acoustics, digital signal processing, audition, the acoustic theory of speech production, and speech perception. The remaining four chapters survey major classes of speech sounds, reviewing their acoustic attributes, as predicted by the acoustic theory of speech production, their auditory characteristics, and their perceptual attributes. Exercises at the end of each chapter highlight the terms introduced in the chapter (the "sufficient jargon" section), and encourage the reader to apply the concepts introduced in the chapter. Some of the questions serve mainly as review; but many extend to problems or topics not directly addressed in the text. The answers to some of the short-answer questions can be found at the end of the book.

I have also included some covert messages in the text. (1) Sample speech sounds are drawn from a variety of languages and speakers, because the acoustic output of the vocal tract depends only on its size and shape and the aerodynamic noise-producing mechanisms employed. These aspects of speech are determined by anatomy and physiology, so are beyond the reach of cultural or personal habit. (2) This is a book about acoustic *and* auditory phonetics, because standard acoustic analysis tells only partial linguistic truths. The auditory system warps the speech signal in some very interesting ways, and if we want to understand the linguistic significance (or lack of it) of speech acoustics, we must pay attention to the auditory system. This second edition also adds a chapter on speech perception, and some data on speech perception in each of the four chapters on major classes of speech sounds, because the linguistic significance of acoustic phonetics is influenced by cognitive perceptual processing. (3) There are formulas in the book. In fact, some of the exercises at the ends of the chapters require the use of a calculator. This may be a cop-out on my part – the language of mathematics is frequently a lot more elegant than any prose I could think up. In my defense I would say that I use only two basic formulas (for the resonances of tubes that are either closed at both ends or closed at only one end); besides, the really interesting part of acoustic phonetics starts when you get out a calculator. The math in this book (what little there is) is easy. (4) IPA (International Phonetic Association) symbols are used throughout. I have assumed that the reader has at least a passing familiarity with the standard set of symbols used in phonetic transcription

Semi-related stuff in boxes

There are all sorts of interesting topics on the edges of the main topics of the chapters. So the book digresses occasionally in boxes such as this to informally address selected (greatest hit) questions that my students have asked. The topics range from underwater speech to the perception of anti-formants, covering digital numbers and the aerodynamics of freeways along the way. I included these digressions because there is no question so simple that it shouldn't be asked. You may find that some of the most interesting stuff in the book is in the boxes.

CHAPTER 1

Basic Acoustics and Acoustic Filters

1.1 The sensation of sound

Several types of events in the world produce the sensation of sound. Examples include doors slamming, violins, wind, and human voices. All these examples, and any others we could think of, involve movement of some sort. And these movements cause **pressure fluctuations** in the surrounding air (or some other acoustic medium). When pressure fluctuations reach the eardrum, they cause it to move, and the auditory system translates these movements into neural impulses which we experience as sound. Thus, sound is produced when pressure fluctuations impinge upon the eardrum. An acoustic waveform is a record of

Acoustic medium

Normally the pressure fluctuations that are heard as sound are produced in air, but it is also possible for sound to travel through other acoustic media. So, for instance, when you are swimming under water, it is possible to hear muffled shouts of the people above the water, and to hear noise as you blow bubbles in the water. Similarly, gases other than air can transmit pressure fluctuations that cause sound. For example, when you speak after inhaling helium from a balloon, the sound of your voice travels through the helium, making it sound different from normal. These examples illustrate that sound properties depend to a certain extent on the acoustic medium, on how quickly pressure fluctuations travel through the medium, and how resistant the medium is to such fluctuations.

sound-producing pressure fluctuations over time. (Ladefoged, 1996, and Fry, 1979, provide more detailed discussions of the topics covered in this chapter.)

1.2   The propagation of sound

Pressure fluctuations impinging on the eardrum produce the sensation of sound, but sound can travel across relatively long distances. This is because a sound produced at one place sets up a **sound wave** that travels through the acoustic medium. A sound wave is a traveling pressure fluctuation that propagates through any medium that is elastic enough to allow molecules to crowd together and move apart. The wave in a lake after you throw in a stone is an example. The impact of the stone is transmitted over a relatively large distance. The water particles don't travel; the pressure fluctuation does.

A line of people waiting to get into a movie is a useful analogy for a sound wave. When the person at the front of the line moves, a "vacuum" is created between the first person and the next person in the line (the gap between them is increased), so the second person steps forward. Now there is a vacuum between person two and person three, so person three steps forward. Eventually, the last person in the line gets to move; the last person is affected by a movement that occurred at the front of the line, because the pressure fluctuation (the gap in the line) traveled, even though each person in the line moved very little. The analogy is flawed, because in most lines you get to move to the front eventually. To be a proper analogy for sound propagation, we would have to imagine that the first person is shoved back into the second person and that this crowding or increase of pressure (like the vacuum) is transmitted down the line.

Figure 1.2 shows a pressure waveform at the location indicated by the asterisk in figure 1.1. The horizontal axis shows the passage of time, the vertical axis the degree of crowdedness (which in a sound wave corresponds to air pressure). At time 3 there is a sudden drop in crowdedness because person two stepped up and left a gap in the line. At time 4 normal crowdedness is restored when person 3 steps up to fill the gap left by person 2. At time 10 there is a sudden increase in crowdedness as person 2 steps back and bumps into person 3. The graph in figure 1.2 is a way of representing the traveling rarefaction and compression waves shown in figure 1.1. Given a uniform acoustic medium, we could reconstruct figure 1.1 from figure 1.2 (though note the discussion in the next paragraph on sound energy dissipation). Graphs like the one shown in figure 1.2 are more typical in acoustic phonetics, because this is the type of view of a sound wave that is produced by a microphone – it shows amplitude fluctuations as they travel past a particular point in space.

Sound waves lose energy as they travel through air (or any other acoustic medium), because it takes energy to move the molecules. Perhaps you have noticed a similar phenomenon when you stand in a long line. If the first person steps forward, then quickly back, only a few people at the front of the line may be affected, because people further down the line have inertia; they will tolerate

Time	1	2	3	4	5	6	7	8	9	10	11	12	13	14	15
		1	1	1	1	1	1	1							
	1		2	2	2	2	2	2	X	1	1	1	1	1	1
*	2	2		3	3	3	3	3	3	X	2	2	2	2	2
	3	3	3		4	4	4	4	4	4	X	3	3	3	3
	4	4	4	4		5	5	5	5	5	5	X	4	4	4
	5	5	5	5	5		6	6	6	6	6	6	X	5	5
	6	6	6	6	6	6		7	7	7	7	7	7	X	6
	7	7	7	7	7	7	7								7

Figure 1.1 Wave motion in a line of seven people waiting to get into a show. Time is shown across the top of the graph running from earlier (time 1) to later (time 15) in arbitrary units.

An analogy for sound propagation

Figure 1.1 shows seven people (represented by numbers) standing in line to see a show. At time 2 the first person steps forward and leaves a gap in the line. So person two steps forward at time 3, leaving a gap between the second and third persons in the line. The gap travels back through the line until time 8, when everyone in the line has moved forward one step. At time 9 the first person in the line is shoved back into place in the line, bumping into person two (this is symbolized by an X). Naturally enough, person two moves out of person one's way at time 10, and bumps into person three. Just as the gap traveled back through the line, now the collision travels back through the line, until at time 15 everyone is back at their starting points.

We can translate the terms of the analogy to sound propagation. The people standing in line correspond to air molecules, the group of them corresponding to an acoustic medium. The gap between successive people is negative air pressure, or rarefaction, and collisions correspond to positive air pressure, or compression. Zero air pressure (which in sound propagation is the atmospheric pressure) is the normal, or preferred, distance between the people standing in line. The initial movement of person one corresponds to the movement of air particles adjacent to one of the tines of a tuning fork (for example) as the tine moves away from the particle. The movement of the first person at time 9 corresponds to the opposite movement of the tuning fork's tine.

some change in pressure (distance between people) before they actually move in response to the change. Thus the disturbance at the front of the line may not have any effect on the people at the end of a long line. Also, people tend to fidget, so the difference between movement propagated down the line and inherent fidgeting

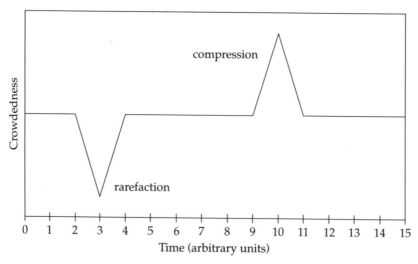

Figure 1.2   A pressure waveform of the wave motion shown in figure 1.1. Time is again shown on the horizontal axis. The vertical axis shows the distance between people.

(the signal-to-noise ratio) may be difficult to detect if the movement is small. The rate of sound dissipation in air is different from the dissipation of a movement in a line, because sound radiates in three dimensions from the sound source (in a sphere). This means that the number of air molecules being moved by the sound wave greatly increases as the wave radiates from the sound source. Thus the amount of energy available to move the molecules (energy per unit surface area on the sphere) decreases as the wave expands out from the sound source, consequently the amount of particle movement decreases as a function of the distance from the sound source (by a power of 3). That is why singers in heavy metal bands put the microphone right up to their lips. They would be drowned out by the general din otherwise. It is also why you should position the microphone close to the speaker's mouth when you record a sample of speech (although it is important to keep the microphone to the side of the speaker's lips, to avoid the blowing noises in [p]'s, etc.).

1.3   Types of sounds

There are two types of sounds: periodic and aperiodic. Periodic sounds have a pattern that repeats at regular intervals. They come in two types: simple and complex.

1.3.1   Simple periodic waves

Simple periodic waves are also called sine waves: they result from simple harmonic motion, such as the swing of a pendulum. The only time we humans get close to producing simple periodic waves in speech is when we're very young. Children's vocal cord vibration comes close to being sinusoidal, and usually women's vocal cord

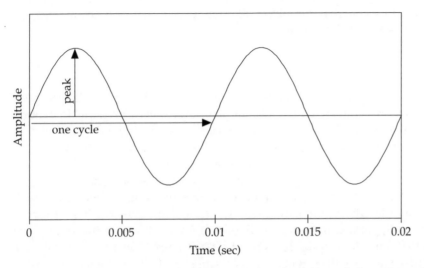

Figure 1.3 A 100 Hz sine wave with the duration of one cycle (the period) and the peak amplitude labeled.

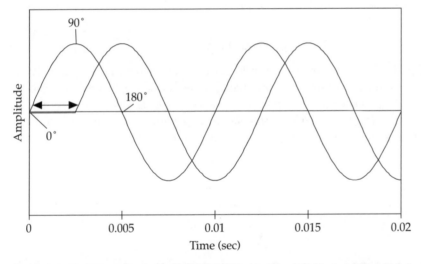

Figure 1.4 Two sine waves with identical frequency and amplitude, but 90° out of phase.

vibration is more sinusoidal than men's. Despite the fact that simple periodic waves rarely occur in speech, they are important, because more complex sounds can be described as combinations of sine waves. In order to define a sine wave, one needs to know just three properties. These are illustrated in figures 1.3–1.4.

The first is frequency: the number of times the sinusoidal pattern repeats per unit time (on the horizontal axis). Each repetition of the pattern is called a cycle, and the duration of a cycle is its period. Frequency can be expressed as cycles per second, which, by convention, is called hertz (and abbreviated Hz). So to get the frequency of a sine wave in Hz (cycles per second), you divide one second by the period (the duration of one cycle). That is, frequency in Hz equals $1/T$, where T

is the period in seconds. For example, the sine wave in figure 1.3 completes one cycle in 0.01 seconds. The number of cycles this wave could complete in one second is 100 (that is, one second divided by the amount of time each cycle takes in seconds, or $1/0.01 = 100$). So, this waveform has a frequency of 100 cycles per second (100 Hz).

The second property of a simple periodic wave is its amplitude: the peak deviation of a pressure fluctuation from normal, atmospheric pressure. In a sound pressure waveform the amplitude of the wave is represented on the vertical axis.

The third property of sine waves is their phase: the timing of the waveform relative to some reference point. You can draw a sine wave by taking amplitude values from a set of right triangles that fit inside a circle (see exercise 4 at the end of this chapter). One time around the circle equals one sine wave on the paper. Thus we can identify locations in a sine wave by degrees of rotation around a circle. This is illustrated in figure 1.4. Both sine waves shown in this figure start at 0° in the sinusoidal cycle. In both, the peak amplitude occurs at 90°, the downward-going (negative-going) zero-crossing at 180°, the negative peak at 270°, and the cycle ends at 360°. But these two sine waves with exactly the same amplitude and frequency may still differ in terms of their relative timing, or phase. In this case they are 90° out of phase.

1.3.2   Complex periodic waves

Complex periodic waves are like simple periodic waves in that they involve a repeating waveform pattern and thus have cycles. However, complex periodic waves are composed of at least two sine waves. Consider the wave shown in figure 1.5, for example. Like the simple sine waves shown in figures 1.3 and 1.4, this waveform completes one cycle in 0.01 seconds (i.e. 10 milliseconds). However,

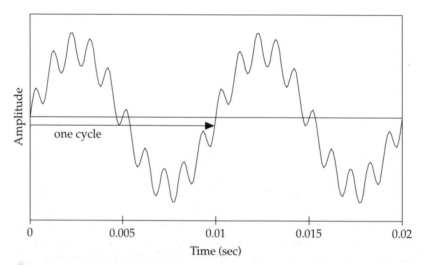

Figure 1.5   A complex periodic wave composed of a 100 Hz sine wave and a 1,000 Hz sine wave. One cycle of the fundamental frequency (F_0) is labeled.

it has an additional component that completes ten cycles in this same amount of time. Notice the "ripples" in the waveform. You can count ten small positive peaks in one cycle of the waveform, one for each cycle of the additional frequency component in the complex wave. I produced this example by adding a 100 Hz sine wave and a (lower-amplitude) 1,000 Hz sine wave. So the 1,000 Hz wave combined with the 100 Hz wave produces a complex periodic wave. The rate at which the complex pattern repeats is called the fundamental frequency (abbreviated F_0).

Fundamental frequency and the GCD

The wave shown in figure 1.5 has a fundamental frequency of 100 Hz and also a 100 Hz component sine wave. It turns out that the fundamental frequency of a complex wave is the greatest common denominator (GCD) of the frequencies of the component sine waves. For example, the fundamental frequency (F_0) of a complex wave with 400 Hz and 500 Hz components is 100 Hz. You can see this for yourself if you draw the complex periodic wave that results from adding a 400 Hz sine wave and a 500 Hz sine wave. We will use the sine wave in figure 1.3 as the starting point for this graph. The procedure is as follows:

1   Take some graph paper.
2   Calculate the period of a 400 Hz sine wave. Because frequency is equal to one divided by the period (in math that's $f = 1/T$), we know that the period is equal to one divided by the frequency ($T = 1/f$). So the period of a 400 Hz sine wave is 0.0025 seconds. In milliseconds (1/1,000ths of a second) that's 2.5 ms (0.0025 times 1,000).
3   Calculate the period of a 500 Hz sine wave.
4   Now we are going to derive two tables of numbers that constitute instructions for drawing 400 Hz and 500 Hz sine waves. To do this, add some new labels to the time axis on figure 1.3, once for the 400 Hz sine wave and once for the 500 Hz sine wave. The 400 Hz time axis will have 2.5 ms in place of 0.01 sec, because the 400 Hz sine wave completes one cycle in 2.5 ms. In place of 0.005 sec the 400 Hz time axis will have 1.25 ms. The peak of the 400 Hz sine wave occurs at 0.625 ms, and the valley at 1.875 ms. This gives us a table of times and amplitude values for the 400 Hz wave (where we assume that the amplitude of the peak is 1 and the amplitude of the valley is –1, and the amplitude value given for time 3.125 is the peak in the second cycle):

ms	0	0.625	1.25	1.875	2.5	3.125
amp	0	1	0	–1	0	1

The interval between successive points in the waveform (with 90° between each point) is 0.625 ms. In the 500 Hz sine wave the interval between comparable points is 0.5 ms.

5   Now on your graph paper mark out 20 ms with 1 ms intervals. Also mark
    an amplitude scale from 1 to –1, allowing about an inch.
6   Draw the 400 Hz and 500 Hz sine waves by marking dots on the graph
    paper for the intersections indicated in the tables. For instance, the first dot
    in the 400 Hz sine wave will be at time 0 ms and amplitude 0, the second at
    time 0.625 ms and amplitude 1, and so on. Note that you may want to extend
    the table above to 20 ms (I stopped at 3.125 to keep the times right for the
    400 Hz wave). When you have marked all the dots for the 400 Hz wave,
    connect the dots with a freehand sine wave. Then draw the 500 Hz sine wave
    in the same way, using the same time and amplitude axes. You should
    have a figure with overlapping sine waves something like figure 1.6.
7   Now add the two waves together. At each 0.5 ms point, take the sum of the
    amplitudes in the two sine waves to get the amplitude value of the new
    complex periodic wave, and then draw the smooth waveform by eye.

Take a look at the complex periodic wave that results from adding a 400 Hz
sine wave and a 500 Hz sine wave. Does it have a fundamental frequency of
100 Hz? If it does, you should see two complete cycles in your 20 ms long
complex wave; the waveform pattern from 10 ms to 20 ms should be an exact
copy of the pattern that you see in the 0 ms to 10 ms interval.

Figure 1.6 shows another complex wave (and four of the sine waves that were
added together to produce it). This wave shape approximates a sawtooth pattern.
Unlike the previous example, it is not possible to identify the component sine
waves by looking at the complex wave pattern. Notice how all four of the component sine waves have positive peaks early in the complex wave's cycle and
negative peaks toward the end of the cycle. These peaks add together to produce
a sharp peak early in the cycle and a sharp valley at the end of the cycle, and
tend to cancel each other over the rest of the cycle. We can't see individual peaks
corresponding to the cycles of the component waves. Nonetheless, the complex
wave *was* produced by adding together simple components.

Now let's look at how to represent the frequency components that make up a
complex periodic wave. What we're looking for is a way to show the component
sine waves of the complex wave when they are not easily visible in the waveform
itself. One way to do this is to list the frequencies and amplitudes of the component sine waves like this:

frequency (Hz)	100	200	300	400	500
amplitude	1	0.5	0.33	0.25	0.2

Figure 1.7 shows a graph of these values with frequency on the horizontal axis and
amplitude on the vertical axis. The graphical display of component frequencies is
the method of choice for showing the simple periodic components of a complex
periodic wave, because complex waves are often composed of so many frequency

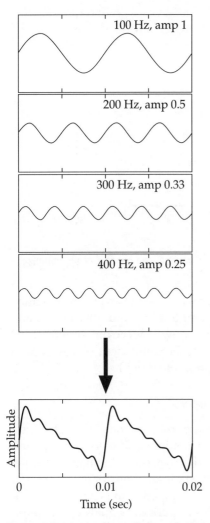

Figure 1.6 A complex periodic wave that approximates the "sawtooth" wave shape, and the four lowest sine waves of the set that were combined to produce the complex wave.

components that a table is impractical. An amplitude versus frequency plot of the simple sine wave components of a complex wave is called a **power spectrum**.

Here's why it is so important that complex periodic waves can be constructed by adding together sine waves. It is possible to produce an infinite variety of complex wave shapes by combining sine waves that have different frequencies, amplitudes, and phases. A related property of sound waves is that any complex acoustic wave can be analyzed in terms of the sine wave components that could have been used to produce that wave. That is, any complex waveform can be decomposed into a set of sine waves having particular frequencies, amplitudes, and phase relations. This property of sound waves is called Fourier's theorem, after the seventeenth-century mathematician who discovered it.

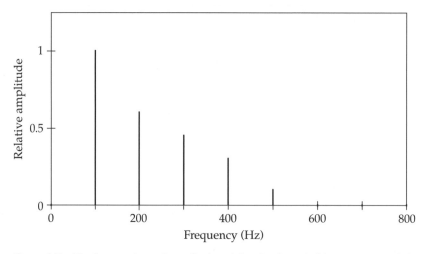

Figure 1.7 The frequencies and amplitudes of the simple periodic components of the complex wave shown in figure 1.6 presented in graphic format.

In Fourier analysis we take a complex periodic wave having an arbitrary number of components and derive the frequencies, amplitudes, and phases of those components. The result of Fourier analysis is a power spectrum similar to the one shown in figure 1.7. (We ignore the phases of the component waves, because these have only a minor impact on the perception of sound.)

1.3.3   Aperiodic waves

Aperiodic sounds, unlike simple or complex periodic sounds, do not have a regularly repeating pattern; they have either a random waveform or a pattern that doesn't repeat. Sound characterized by random pressure fluctuation is called "white noise." It sounds something like radio static or wind blowing through trees. Even though white noise is not periodic, it is possible to perform a Fourier analysis on it; however, unlike Fourier analyses of periodic signals composed of only a few sine waves, the spectrum of white noise is not characterized by sharp peaks, but, rather, has equal amplitude for all possible frequency components (the spectrum is flat). Like sine waves, white noise is an abstraction, although many naturally occurring sounds are similar to white noise. For instance, the sound of the wind or fricative speech sounds like [s] or [f].

Figures 1.8 and 1.9 show the acoustic waveform and the power spectrum, respectively, of a sample of white noise. Note that the waveform shown in figure 1.8 is irregular, with no discernible repeating pattern. Note too that the spectrum shown in figure 1.9 is flat across the top. As we noted earlier, a Fourier analysis of a short chunk (called an "analysis window") of a waveform leads to inaccuracies in the resultant spectrum. That's why this spectrum has some peaks and valleys even though, according to theory, white noise should have a flat spectrum.

The other main type of aperiodic sounds are **transients**. These are various types of clanks and bursts which produce a sudden pressure fluctuation that is not

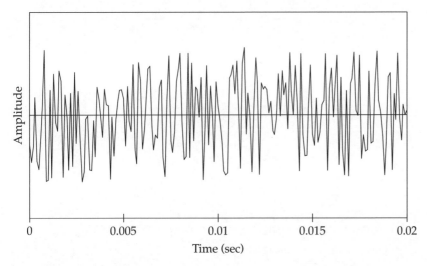

Figure 1.8 A 20 ms section of an acoustic waveform of white noise. The amplitude at any given point in time is random.

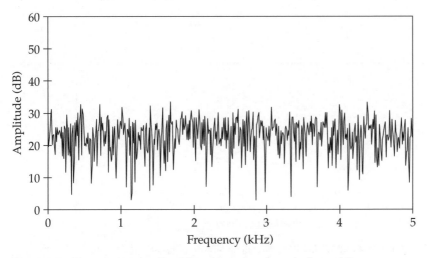

Figure 1.9 The power spectrum of the white noise shown in figure 1.8.

sustained or repeated over time. Door slams, balloon pops, and electrical clicks are all transient sounds. Like aperiodic noise, transient sounds can be analyzed into their spectral components using Fourier analysis. Figure 1.10 shows an idealized transient signal. At only one point in time is there any energy in the signal; at all other times pressure is equal to zero. This type of idealized sound is called an "impulse." Naturally occurring transients approximate the shape of an impulse, but usually with a bit more complicated fluctuation. Figure 1.11 shows the power spectrum of the impulse shown in figure 1.10. As with white noise, the spectrum is flat. This is more obvious in figure 1.11 than in figure 1.9 because the "impulseness" of the impulse waveform depends on only one point in time, while the "white noiseness"

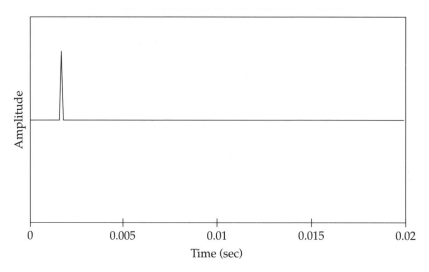

Figure 1.10   Acoustic waveform of a transient sound (an impulse).

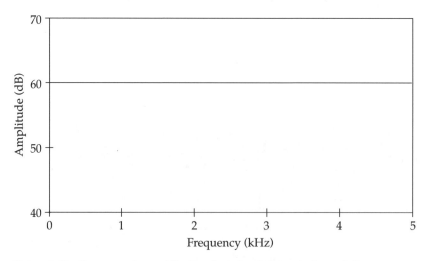

Figure 1.11   Power spectrum of the transient signal shown in figure 1.10.

of the white noise waveform depends on every point in time. Thus, because the Fourier analysis is only approximately valid for a short sample of a waveform, the white noise spectrum is not as completely specified as is the impulse spectrum.

1.4   Acoustic filters

We are all familiar with how filters work. For example, you use a paper filter to keep the coffee grounds out of your coffee, or a tea ball to keep the tea leaves out of your tea. These everyday examples illustrate some important properties of acoustic filters. For instance, the practical difference between a coffee filter and a

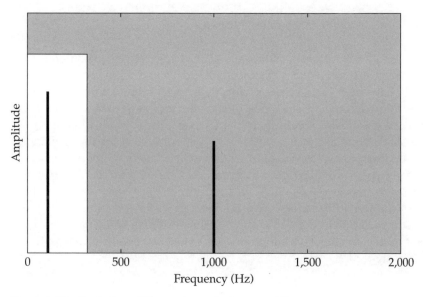

Figure 1.12   Illustration of the spectrum of a low-pass filter.

tea ball is that the tea ball will allow larger bits into the drink, while the coffee filter captures smaller particles than does the tea ball. So the difference between these filters can be described in terms of the size of particles they let pass.

Rather than passing or blocking particles of different sizes like a coffee filter, an acoustic filter passes or blocks components of sound of different frequencies. For example, a **low-pass** acoustic filter blocks the high-frequency components of a wave, and passes the low-frequency components. Earlier I illustrated the difference between simple and complex periodic waves by adding a 1,000 Hz sine wave to a 100 Hz sine wave to produce a complex wave. With a low-pass filter that, for instance, filtered out all frequency components above 300 Hz, we could remove the 1,000 Hz wave from the complex wave. Just as a coffee filter allows small particles to pass through and blocks large particles, so a low-pass acoustic filter allows low-frequency components through, but blocks high-frequency components.

You can visualize the action of a low-pass filter in a spectral display of the filter's response function. For instance, figure 1.12 shows a low-pass filter that has a cutoff frequency of 300 Hz. The part of the spectrum shaded white is called the **pass band**, because sound energy in this frequency range is passed by the filter, while the part of the spectrum shaded gray is called the **reject band**, because sound energy in this region is blocked by the filter. Thus, in a complex wave with components at 100 and 1,000 Hz, the 100 Hz component is passed, and the 1,000 Hz component is blocked. Similarly, a **high-pass** acoustic filter blocks the low-frequency components of a wave, and passes the high-frequency components. A spectral display of the response function of a high-pass filter shows that low-frequency components are blocked by the filter, and high-frequency components are passed.

Filter slopes

The low-pass filter illustrated in figure 1.12 has a very sharp boundary at 300 Hz between the frequencies that are blocked by the filter and those that are passed. The filter has the same effect on every component below (or above) the cutoff frequency; the slope of the vertical line separating the pass band from the reject band is infinitely steep. In real life, acoustic filters do not have such sharp boundaries. For instance, it is more typical for the transition between pass band and reject band to extend over some range of frequencies (as in the band-pass filter illustrated in figure 1.13), rather than to occur instantaneously (as in the low-pass filter illustration). A very steep slope is like having very uniform-sized holes in a tea ball. A shallow filter slope is like having lots of variation in the size of the holes in a tea ball. Some particles will be blocked by the smaller holes, though they would have got through if they had found a bigger hole.

Band-pass filters are important, because we can model some aspects of articulation and hearing in terms of the actions of band-pass filters. Unlike low-pass or high-pass filters, which have a single cutoff frequency, band-pass filters have two cutoff frequencies, one for the low end of the pass band and one for the high end of the pass band (as figure 1.13 shows). A band-pass filter is like a combination of

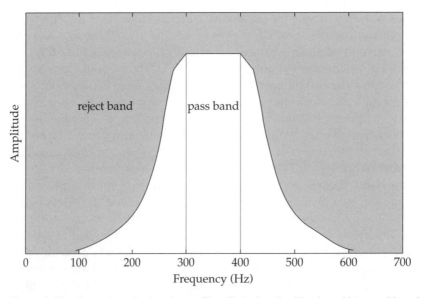

Figure 1.13 Illustration of a band-pass filter. Note that the filter has skirts on either side of the pass band.

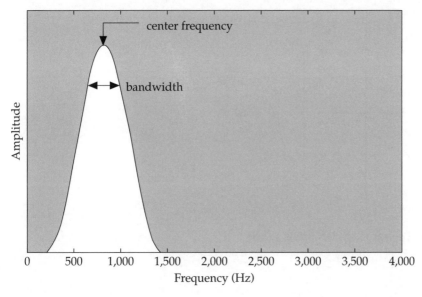

Figure 1.14 A band-pass filter described by the center frequency and bandwidth of the filter.

a low-pass filter and a high-pass filter, where the cutoff frequency of the low-pass filter is higher than the cutoff frequency of the high-pass filter.

When the high and low cutoff frequencies of a band-pass filter equal each other, the resulting filter can be characterized by its **center frequency** and the filter's **bandwidth** (which is determined by the slopes of the filter). Bandwidth is the width (in Hz) of the filter's peak such that one-half of the acoustic energy in the filter is within the stated width. That is, considering the total area under the curve of the filter shape, the bandwidth is the range, around the center frequency, that encloses half the total area. In practice, this half-power bandwidth is found by measuring the amplitude at the center frequency of the filter and then finding the width of the filter at an amplitude that is three decibels (dB) below the peak amplitude (a decibel is defined in chapter 3). This special type of band-pass filter, which is illustrated in figure 1.14, is important in acoustic phonetics, because it has been used to model the filtering action of the vocal tract and auditory system.

Exercises

Sufficient jargon

Define the following terms: sound, acoustic medium, acoustic waveform, sound wave, compression, rarefaction, periodic sounds, simple periodic wave, sine wave, frequency, Hertz, cycle, period, amplitude, phase, complex periodic wave, fundamental frequency, component waves, power spectrum, Fourier's theorem, Fourier analysis, aperiodic sounds, white noise, transient, impulse, low-pass filter, pass band, reject band, high-pass filter, filter slope, band-pass filter, center frequency, bandwidth.

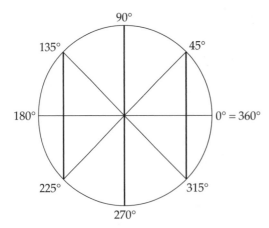

Figure 1.15   Degrees of rotation around a circle.

Short-answer questions

1   What's wrong with this statement: You experience sound when air molecules move from a sound source to your eardrum.
2   Express these times in seconds: 1,000 ms, 200 ms, 10 ms, 1,210 ms.
3   What is the frequency in Hz if the period of a sine wave is 0.01 sec, 10 ms, 0.33 sec, 33 ms?
4   Draw a sine wave. First, draw a time axis in equal steps of size 45, so that the first label is zero, the next one (to the right) is 45, the next is 90, and so on up to 720. These labels refer to the degrees of rotation around a circle, as shown in figure 1.15 (720° is twice around the circle). Now plot amplitude values in the sine wave as the height of the vertical bars in the figure relative to the line running through the center of the circle from 0° to 180°. So the amplitude value at 0° is 0; the amplitude at 45° is the vertical distance from the center line to the edge of the circle at 45°, and so on. If the line descends from the center line (as is the case for 225°), mark the amplitude as a negative value. Now connect the dots freehand, trying to make your sine wave look like the ones in this chapter (don't use your ruler for this).
5   Draw the waveform of the complex wave produced by adding sine waves of 300 Hz and 500 Hz (both with peak amplitude of 1).
6   Draw the spectrum of a complex periodic wave composed of 100 Hz and 700 Hz components (both with peak amplitude of 1).
7   Draw the spectrum of an acoustic filter that results from adding two band-pass filters. Filter 1 has a center frequency of 500 Hz and a bandwidth of 50 Hz, while filter 2 has a center frequency of 1,500 Hz and a bandwidth of 150 Hz.

CHAPTER 2

Digital Signal Processing

The instrumentation used in acoustic phonetics has changed dramatically in the last couple of decades. Now, rather than oscilloscopes, chart recorders, and spectrographs, we use computers and computer programs almost exclusively. This chapter discusses digital signal processing – the way that computers handle acoustic signals. The goal of this chapter is to give you an intuitive grasp of how computers perform acoustic analysis. This material may also be of interest because we will be discussing some terms that you may have heard in connection with compact disc players and computer sound cards. (I highly recommend Richard Lyons' 1997 book for further discussion of the material covered in this chapter.)

2.1 Continuous versus discrete signals

An understanding of digital signal processing (DSP) starts with the dichotomy between **continuous** and **discrete** signals. This dichotomy concerns the way in which time and amplitude are represented in a waveform. Figure 2.1 illustrates the difference between continuous and discrete signals (the two signals are slightly phase-shifted, in order to make it easier to see them both). As the figure illustrates, a continuous signal is best represented as a continuous line having an amplitude value at all points in time, while a discrete signal is actually a sequence of separate amplitude values, and thus is most accurately represented by separate (discrete) points rather than a line. In a continuous signal, time and amplitude are represented by numbers that have a theoretically infinite number of places after the decimal point. So we might measure the amplitude of a signal as 3.211178 . . . volts at time 1.00333483 . . . seconds. In discrete signals the number of decimal places (for both time and amplitude) is always limited.

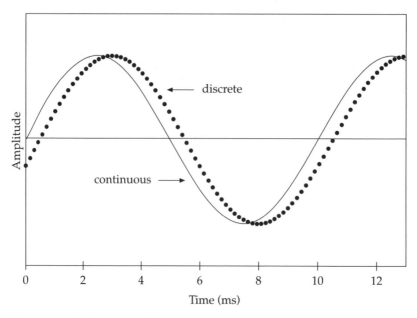

Figure 2.1   Continuous and discrete sine waves.

Many of the instruments that we use in recording and analyzing speech can convert continuous air pressure variations into continuous electrical signals, but computers can't do this. Computers can't store numbers with an infinite number of places after the decimal point, so all acoustic signals in computers are discrete, even though the pressure fluctuations that produce the sensation of sound are always continuous. Instruments like tape recorders that can store a continuous signal are called "analog devices," because they can store electric analogs of the acoustic signal, whereas instruments that have to convert the continuous speech signal into a discrete signal are called "digital devices," because signals get stored as digits. So, the terms **analog** and **digital** are synonyms for continuous and discrete. Note, however, that analog devices are not necessarily better at storing and analyzing sounds. If you retain enough decimal places when you convert a continuous signal to digital format, all the auditorily important information can be captured (as, for example, in compact discs).

2.2   Analog-to-digital conversion

For a computer to "record" speech, it is necessary to convert the continuous sound wave into a discrete signal that can be stored (and manipulated) by the computer. This is done by a two-step process called analog-to-digital conversion. In the first step, we limit the number of places after the decimal point on the time axis; so, rather than have infinitely many points in time, the continuous signal is chopped up into a sequence of **samples**, or discrete points in time. In the second step, we limit the number of places after the decimal point on the amplitude axis; so, rather than have infinitely many possible levels of amplitude, the signal is **quantized**. In order to get an accurate digital representation of an acoustic signal, we have to pay attention to some potential problems in both the sampling and the quantization stages of analog-to-digital conversion.

An illustration of analog-to-digital conversion

Analog-to-digital conversion is like converting the graph of a sine wave into a table of numbers, using a ruler to take measurements of the waveform. First, you mark off equal intervals on the time axis, and then at each tick on the time axis you take a measurement of the amplitude of the wave. Marking intervals on the time axis corresponds to **sampling**, which is discussed in section 2.2.1, and measuring the amplitude of the waveform at each time point corresponds to **quantization**, which is discussed in section 2.2.2.

2.2.1   Sampling

The main thing we have to pay attention to in the sampling stage of analog-to-digital conversion is the sampling rate. It is important to sample the signal often enough to capture all the information that is important for listeners. Suppose we have a sine wave that repeats 100 times per second (100 Hz). How many samples per second do we need to take (assuming that the time interval between samples is constant) in order to capture the fact that there is a 100 Hz periodic wave? As figure 2.2 shows, it is necessary to have *at least* two samples for each cycle of the sine wave in order to capture the periodicity. Of course, we have to

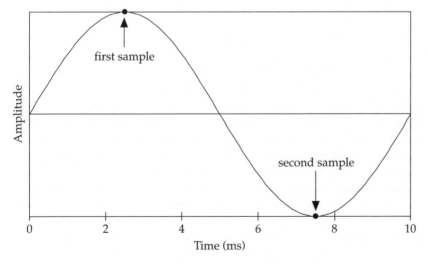

Figure 2.2   This figure illustrates why it takes two samples to capture the periodicity of a sine wave.

have a lot more samples to capture the specific wave shape (sine versus square, for example), but two samples per cycle is enough to tell us that there is a component at that frequency. So, to capture a 100 Hz periodic component in a continuous wave, the discrete representation of that wave has to have at least two samples for each cycle. That is, we must take samples 200 times per second. Another way to say this is that the sampling rate must be at least 200 Hz.

A term that often comes up in this context is **Nyquist frequency**. This is the highest-frequency component that can be captured with a given sampling rate. In the example given above, with a sampling rate of 200 Hz, the Nyquist frequency is 100 Hz. The Nyquist frequency is always one-half the sampling rate.

DSP and CDs

If you've been shopping for a stereo system recently, you may remember that manufacturers often claim that their loudspeakers are responsive from 20 Hz to 20,000 Hz. They choose this range of frequencies because it represents the lower and upper limits of the range of frequencies that we can hear (actually, as people get older, their sensitivity to high frequencies usually decreases, and 20,000 Hz is the upper limit for young healthy ears). Because we know that the sampling rate in analog-to-digital conversion has to be twice the frequency of any spectral component that we want to capture, then if we want to capture all audible frequencies (any sound from 20 to 20,000 Hz), we must use a sampling rate of about 40,000 Hz. That's why digital audio devices like CD players use a sampling rate of 44,000 Hz.

There is a trade-off between sampling rate and the amount of storage space that a sound wave occupies in a computer. If we sample at 40,000 Hz (40 kHz), then we have to store 40,000 samples for every second of speech recorded. Most computers will run out of space pretty quickly at this rate, so we would like to be able to use a lower sampling rate. The frequency range of the telephone is "band-limited," so that only frequency components above 300 Hz and below 4,000 Hz are transmitted. This is a holdover from the time when carbon-button micro-phones, which had this kind of frequency response, were used. It means that we could sample speech at a rate of 8,000 samples per second (8 kHz), and get speech that is as intelligible as speech over the telephone. However, as figure 2.3 shows, some speech sounds (like [s]) usually have significant amounts of energy at frequencies above 4,000 Hz. Previous research on the acoustic phonetic de-scription of speech sounds suggests that they do not have significant amounts of information in frequencies above 10 kHz. Consequently, a sampling rate of about 20 kHz is adequate for recording speech sounds. Evidently the stereo-maker's choice to design an audio system for "young healthy" ears is overkill for speech communication. One factor that may account for this is that speech communica-tion involves a wide spectrum of speakers (old and young), and occurs in a wide

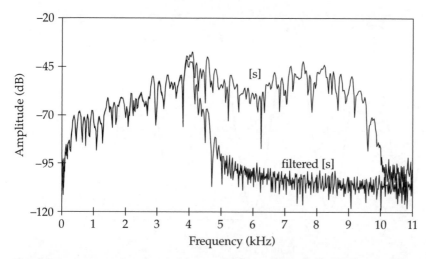

Figure 2.3   Power spectra of [s] showing that this sound has relatively high-amplitude spectral components above 4 kHz. The spectra are identical up to about 4 kHz. The waveform of the spectrum labeled "filtered [s]" was run through a low-pass filter with a cutoff frequency of 4 kHz. That labeled "[s]" was also filtered, but with a low-pass filter having a cutoff frequency of 9 kHz.

variety of environments (some of them rather noisy). As we shall see in the next chapter, frequency components above 10 kHz are not likely to be useful for speech communication even if the listener has perfect hearing, because human sensitivity to frequency information above 10 kHz is rather limited. So, rather than sample speech at 40 kHz and try to store all those samples on disk, I use a system that samples speech at 22 kHz.

Figure 2.4 illustrates another problem in going from a continuous signal to a discrete signal. Here we have a continuous sine wave that oscillates too quickly to be adequately represented by the discrete samples. The frequency of the continuous signal is greater than half the sampling rate (the Nyquist frequency); consequently the discrete sampled waveform has a completely different frequency from the original continuous signal. The problem is that the continuous signal completes more than one cycle between successive digital samples, so it looks as if the samples were taken from a wave with a much lower frequency. This misrepresentation of a continuous signal in a discrete waveform is called **aliasing**, and it occurs when the continuous signal contains frequency components that are higher than half the sampling rate. To avoid aliasing, we must either increase the sampling rate to capture all the frequency components in the analog signal or filter out all frequencies above half the sampling rate. Because in naturally occurring signals (as opposed to pure sine waves) there are always very high-frequency components, it is *always* necessary to filter out frequencies above half the chosen sampling rate.

As already discussed, it is possible to capture all of the auditorily important information in the speech signal by choosing a sampling rate of about 20 kHz, because that captures all the frequency components in the signal from 0 to 10 kHz.

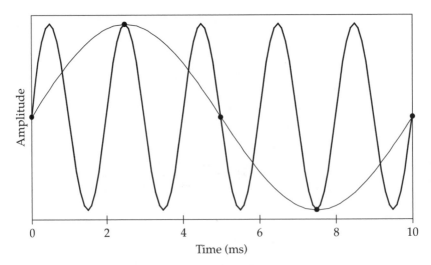

Time (ms)

Figure 2.4 An illustration of aliasing in analog-to-digital conversion. The analog signal (heavy line) oscillates too quickly to be accurately represented by the samples in the digital signal (indicated by the solid dots). Therefore the digital signal contains a low-frequency component (light line), rather than an accurate representation of the high-frequency input signal.

As figure 2.4 illustrates, however, any component with a frequency higher than 10 kHz will not only not be captured in the digital waveform; it will corrupt it by introducing alias components into the discrete signal. Therefore, it is necessary to use a low-pass filter to block all the frequency components in the continuous signal that will produce alias components. This is called an **anti-aliasing** filter. If we choose a sampling rate of 20 kHz, the anti-aliasing filter will need to block all the frequency components above 10 kHz and pass all the frequency components below 10 kHz. Because real-life filter slopes are not infinitely steep, we would actually use a low-pass filter with a cutoff frequency of about 7 or 7.5 kHz for a sampling rate of 20 kHz. That way we can be assured that the alias-causing frequency components will be blocked by the filter. The equipment that I use has a sampling rate of 22 kHz and a low-pass filter with a cutoff frequency of 9 kHz. CD players low-pass filter the signal at 20 kHz and sample at 44 kHz. (Usage note: "low-pass filter" can be used as a noun or a verb. So we can say either "use a low-pass filter with a cutoff frequency of 7.5 kHz" or "low-pass filter the signal at 7.5 kHz.") This low-pass anti-aliasing filtering prior to analog-to-digital conversion is absolutely essential, otherwise the digital signal contains spurious frequency components that were not present in the original continuous signal.

2.2.2   Quantization

After we've chopped up a continuous signal into discrete samples, we have to measure the amplitude of the signal at each of those points in time. This stage in

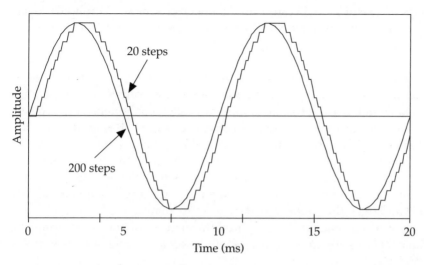

Figure 2.5 An illustration of two different quantization schemes. In the sine wave labeled "20 steps," amplitude is represented as one of 20 possible values. In that labeled "200 steps," amplitude of the same sine wave is represented as one of 200 possible values. The sine waves are phase-shifted slightly, to make the comparison more easily visible.

analog-to-digital conversion, quantization, is directly analogous to measuring the amplitudes in the waveform with a ruler.

The main issue we have to consider in quantization is the accuracy of the amplitude measurements. This issue comes up when you measure amplitude using a ruler. Will you round off the measurements to the nearest $\frac{1}{4}$ inch, or should you take the extra effort to measure to the nearest $\frac{1}{8}$ inch? Figure 2.5 illustrates the effect of choosing two different measurement scales. In one case, amplitude is represented as one of 20 possible values, while in the other, there are 200 possible amplitude values. (To make this graph I rounded off the numbers produced by the sine function, which vary continuously from 1 to −1, to either one place after the decimal (0, 0.1, etc.) to get the 20-step quantization or two places after the decimal (0, 0.01, 0.02, etc.) to get the 200-step quantization.) As figure 2.5 shows, a smooth continuous waveform can end up looking jagged if the amplitude is not measured accurately enough. In this section we will discuss briefly what is meant by "accurately enough."

To define "accurately enough," we need a unit of measure. To quantize a printed waveform, we choose a unit of measure like inches or millimeters in order to define "accurately enough"; similarly, there are several ways of measuring quantization accuracy in computerized analog-to-digital conversion. For instance, we could define "accurately enough" in terms of sound pressure, or in terms of volts produced by a microphone. However, both of these possible units of measure are too far removed from the process of quantization to be of much practical utility. In practice, we define the accuracy of quantization in terms of the number of separate amplitude levels that can be represented digitally in a computer. (The ruler analogy is useful here, because the "number of separate amplitude levels that can be represented" is analogous to measurement using $\frac{1}{4}$-inch marks or $\frac{1}{16}$-inch marks. The accuracy of the measurement depends on how many divisions are available.) Because computers can handle integers (1, 2, 3, etc.) much more efficiently than floating-point numbers (0.01, 0.02, 0.03, etc.), and the process of quantization involves reducing a continuous amplitude scale to a discrete scale with a countable number of possible amplitude values, computers store acoustic waveforms as a sequence of integers. For instance., in the 20-step quantization illustrated in figure 2.5, rather than store the floating-point numbers 0.8, 0.9, etc., a computer would store integers ranging from 1 to 20 (or if you prefer, −10 to 10). Also, the potential size of an integer is determined by the number of binary digits (bits) that are used to represent it in the computer's memory (see box on **digital numbers**). The larger the number of bits used to represent each sample in a digital waveform, the greater the amplitude resolution of the waveform. The most popular choices for the number of bits used to encode speech samples are 8, 12, and 16.

Digital numbers

Computers use sequences of 1s and 0s to encode information. The number of these binary digits (bits) used to encode a number determines the maximum value the number can take, and thus, in a digital waveform, the degree of amplitude resolution that can be captured. For example, a two-bit number can be one of four different combinations of 1 and 0 (00, 01, 10, 11). The integers associated with these combinations are: 00 = 0, 01 = 1, 10 = 2, 11 = 3. So, with two-bit numbers, a computer can count from 0 to 3. A three-bit number can be one of eight combinations of 1s and 0s, standing for the integers from 0 to 7. And a four-bit number can be one of $2^4 = 16$ different combinations of 1s and 0s, standing for the integers from 0 to 15. In this way the number of bits used to store numbers in a computer corresponds to the scale on a ruler; consequently, the accuracy of quantization in analog-to-digital conversion is usually defined in terms of the number of bits used to store waveform samples.

The process of analog-to-digital conversion introduces a certain amount of error into the digital signal by virtue of the fact that a continuous signal is being represented as a discrete signal. Figure 2.6 illustrates this fact. The figure shows a continuous waveform, a discrete representation of it (using 20 amplitude steps), and a waveform showing the difference between the continuous and discrete waveforms. This third waveform shows the **quantization noise** in the discrete waveform. Any digital waveform contains some degree of quantization noise, because in digital waveforms the signal jumps from one quantization step to the next, rather than following the continuous signal at all possible points in time. Quantization noise is quasi-random (sort of like white noise), and varies over a

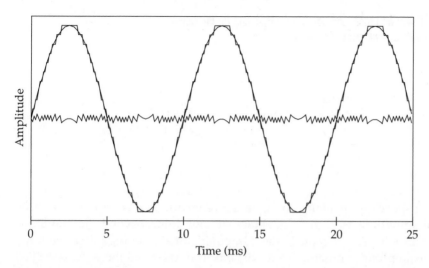

Figure 2.6 An illustration of quantization noise. Continuous and discrete representations of a sine wave are shown (in phase, so they are on top of each other). The somewhat random signal oscillating around zero amplitude is the difference between the two representations: the quantization noise.

range from $-\frac{1}{2}$ to $\frac{1}{2}$ amplitude steps. That is, the amplitude in the continuous waveform is always between $-\frac{1}{2}$ and $\frac{1}{2}$ an amplitude step from the amplitude that is recorded in the discrete waveform (provided an adequate anti-aliasing filter is used). You can sometimes hear quantization noise when you play out a digital sound (especially with eight-bit quantization). The best way to avoid it is to use a large number of amplitude steps (compare the 20-step trace to the 200-step trace in figure 2.5). The amplitude of quantization noise can be usefully expressed by comparing it with the maximum possible amplitude of the signal. If we have 256 amplitude steps (eight-bit samples), the ratio of the maximum amplitude of the signal to the amplitude of the quantization noise is 256:1, but with twelve-bit samples the ratio is 4,096:1, and with sixteen-bit samples is 65,536:1. Clearly, the relative loudness of quantization noise (the signal-to-noise ratio) is lower when we use more bits to store the signal (this is why CD players use sixteen-bit quantization).

It used to be the case that researchers would choose 8-bit quantization for large audio data sets that they wanted to distribute (on floppy disks!). More commonly now, large datasets are distributed in 16-bit format on CD-ROMs or over the web. Data compression is also commonly used to reduce the sizes of audio files to be distributed. So, it is important to keep in mind the difference between lossy and loss-less data compression. Lossy compression schemes remove information, so that the original digital acoustic waveform cannot be restored from the compressed file. MP3, for example, is a lossy compression scheme, which is why MP3 recordings don't sound as good as the original (and why the whole Napster thing was odd). Table 2.1 compares lossy and loss-less compression schemes.

Table 2.1   Lossy and loss-less compression standards for visual images, audio data, and computer files.

	lossy	loss-less
Visual images	JPEG	GIF
Audio data	MPEG, RealAudio	ADPCM
Files		ZIP, TAR

Finally, because the amplitude of quantization noise is constant, the amplitude of the signal determines the signal-to-noise ratio. Therefore, when digitizing speech (converting speech from analog to digital representation), it is important to keep the signal amplitude as high as possible, without going beyond the amplitude that the computer can accept. If the computer's analog-to-digital converter is sensitive to amplitudes ranging from −10 volts to 10 volts and the signal supplied to the computer ranges only from −5 volts to 5 volts, then the digital signal will have a relatively higher quantization noise than if you had amplified the signal properly. In this example, with an eight-bit analog-to-digital converter, by using only half the available input voltage range, we use only seven of the eight possible bits to store each sample, and thus the signal-to-noise ratio is 128:1 rather than 256:1. The signal-to-noise ratio is usually less of an issue with sixteen-bit analog-to-digital converters, because the level of quantization noise is quite low in sixteen-bit sampling, but signal-to-noise ratio should never be ignored when digitizing speech. Note one caution though: bad things happen when the input volume goes beyond the range that can be represented in the digital waveform. This is called **clipping**. Clipping introduces transients in the digital waveform, and as a result messes up any spectral analysis that you then try to perform on the signal (see the transient spectrum in figure 1.12).

2.3   Signal analysis methods

This section discusses six DSP analysis techniques that are commonly used in acoustic phonetics. My goal is to present some basic information about these techniques, so that you will know how to set the analysis parameters in your computer speech analysis program. Consequently, this is a practical introduction to the methods, rather than the more detailed mathematical description that you will find in O'Shaughnessy (1987) or other engineering introductions.

2.3.1   Auto-correlation pitch tracking

Figure 2.7 shows that if you overlay successive periods of a complex wave, they will show a high degree of correlation; that is, the waveform is correlated with itself. Take a copy of the waveform from the point labeled "misaligned" in figure 2.7, and line it up with the start of the original waveform as the arrow indicates and

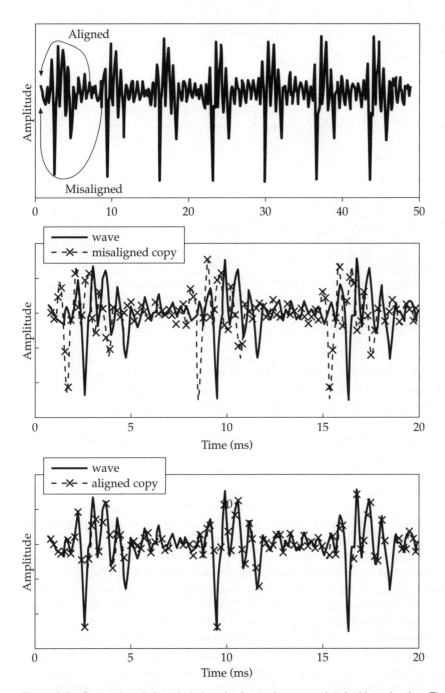

Figure 2.7 Successive pitch periods in voiced speech are correlated with each other. The top panel shows 50 milliseconds of the Cherokee vowel [ʌ]. The middle panel shows the result when we plot the original waveform and a misaligned copy. The bottom panel shows the result when we plot the original waveform with a copy that is offset from the original by exactly one pitch period.

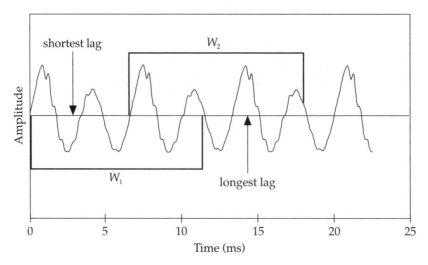

Figure 2.8 An illustration of the auto-correlation method of pitch tracking. The second window (W_2) is offset from the first (W_1) by a series of different "lag" values ranging from "shortest lag" to "longest lag." The duration of the pitch period is considered to be the lag duration for which the correlation between the waveform in W_1 and the waveform in W_2 is highest.

the two waveforms do not correspond (as shown in the middle panel). But, if we get the alignment right, so that the copy starts exactly one pitch period into the duration of the original (labeled "aligned" in the figure), then the two waveforms correspond almost exactly (bottom panel). The auto-correlation technique for pitch estimation uses this property of voiced speech to automatically find the fundamental frequency (F_0) of the waveform. A "pitch track" shows estimates of the F_0 of vocal fold vibration as a function of time, where new estimates are calculated at intervals of 10 or 20 ms. The method takes a small chunk from the acoustic waveform (a waveform "window"), usually several periods long, and calculates correlations over a range of possible period lengths, reporting the period length that produced the highest correlation.

Figure 2.8 illustrates the auto-correlation method of pitch tracking. This figure shows two overlapping windows (waveform chunks) in a complex periodic wave. The complex waves in these two windows are highly correlated with each other, because the interval between the start of W_1 and the start of W_2 – the "lag" – is exactly the duration of one cycle. In order to find the pitch period, the auto-correlation method calculates the correlation between W_1 and W_2 for every lag time between the points labeled "shortest lag" and "longest lag." That is, it positions W_2 to start at "shortest lag," calculates the correlation between W_1 and W_2, then moves W_2 to the right one sample in the digital waveform and calculates the correlation again; it continues to shift W_2 to the right until the starting point of the window is equal to "longest lag." The lag duration with the highest correlation between W_1 and W_2 is considered to be the duration of one period. The inverse of this duration is the fundamental frequency of the complex wave (e.g. let T equal the duration of one period in seconds, then the F_0 in Hz is equal to $1/T$).

One way to speed up the auto-correlation method is to restrict the range of possible pitch periods considered; in this way you limit the number of correlations that have to be calculated. Many computer speech analysis packages do this by using an estimate of the speaker's average F_0 or a range of possible F_0 values. These are usually parameters that the user can modify, and in many cases should modify, for particular speakers. Two very common errors are made by auto-correlation pitch trackers: pitch-halving and pitch-doubling. Both these errors can occur even if the F_0 range expected by the program is correct; but one or the other is guaranteed to occur if the program's parameters are set incorrectly.

Pitch-halving occurs when two pitch periods can fit into the windows W_1 and W_2 (figure 2.8) and the "shortest lag" comes after the end of the first pitch period in W_1. In this situation, the pitch tracker is expecting pitch periods to be longer than those actually occurring in the signal; consequently the best correlation that it finds is when W_2 starts at the beginning of the third pitch period in the analysis interval (rather than the normal situation in which the best correlation is found when W_2 starts at the beginning of the second pitch period in the analysis interval, as shown in figure 2.8). When W_2 starts at the beginning of the third pitch period, the lag value is equal to the duration of two pitch periods, so the reported F_0 is one-half the actual F_0. Pitch-halving can also occur even when the expected F_0 range is correct. This usually happens when alternating pitch periods are more similar than adjacent pitch periods, as in some phonation types, including vocal fry and diplophonia.

Pitch-doubling occurs when the shortest lag analyzed is as short as half a pitch period, and the second half of the period looks very much like the first half. This is illustrated in figure 2.8, where each period in the waveform can be divided into two very similar-looking halves; each period is composed of a positive peak followed by a negative peak and then a second positive peak followed by a second negative peak. The auto-correlation method can easily be convinced that the two halves of each cycle are separate cycles, and will invariably give this erroneous result if the "longest lag" value is less than one full pitch period. When half a pitch period is mistakenly identified as the period duration, the reported F_0 value is double the actual value.

2.3.2   RMS amplitude

The amplitude of a waveform can be measured in several ways, as illustrated in figure 2.9. In simple periodic (sine) waves, the three methods – peak amplitude, peak-to-peak amplitude, and root mean square (RMS) amplitude – can be mathematically derived from each other. For instance, the peak-to-peak amplitude is twice the peak amplitude, and RMS amplitude taken over one cycle of a sine wave is equal to the peak amplitude multiplied by 0.707. For complex waves the different measures of amplitude are not mutually predictable. The peak measurements differ from RMS amplitude in that they give a measure of acoustic amplitude, whereas RMS amplitude is a measure of acoustic intensity. Because perceived loudness is more closely tied to acoustic intensity than to acoustic amplitude, most speech analysis packages will calculate and report RMS amplitude automatically.

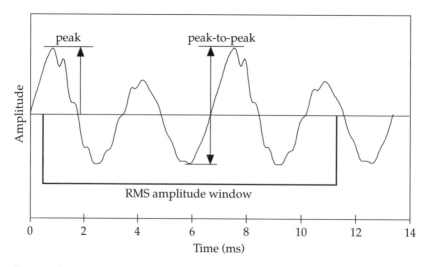

Figure 2.9 Two periods of a vowel waveform showing three types of amplitude measurements: peak amplitude, peak-to-peak amplitude, and a window over which RMS amplitude may be calculated.

To calculate RMS amplitude, each sample in a waveform window is squared; then the average of the squares is calculated; and finally, the square root is taken. The procedure is outlined in the name: the root of the mean of the squared samples. For example, if we have a window of nine samples $(0, 3, 5, 2, 0, -3, -5, -2, 0)$, the squared samples are $(0, 9, 25, 4, 0, 9, 25, 4, 0)$, the average of the squares is $76/9 = 8.44$, and the square root (the RMS amplitude) is 2.9. Note that a waveform with exactly the same peak amplitude as this but a higher frequency $(0, 5, 0, -5, 0, 5, 0, -5, 0)$ has a higher RMS amplitude $(\sqrt{(100/9)} = 3.33)$. Also, the RMS amplitude of complex waves with different wave shapes may differ, while their peak amplitudes do not. For example, $(0, 0, 5, 0, 0, 0, -5, 0, 0)$ has a lower RMS amplitude (2.36) than the first example given, even though the frequency is the same.

RMS amplitude is used in many speech analysis programs to produce an "amplitude trace" analogous to a pitch trace. This is a plot of amplitude measurements taken from successive or overlapping windows in the speech signal.

There are two practical considerations to be aware of when selecting the window size for RMS (if your analysis program allows you to vary the window size). First, longer windows result in smoother amplitude curves. For instance, if the window size is 20 ms or longer, then because each RMS measurement involves averaging squared samples over the duration of the window, glottal pulses will not show up as separate peaks in the amplitude trace. However – and this is the second practical consideration – the temporal accuracy of the amplitude trace is reduced when a long analysis window is used. As the window size increases, the ability of the RMS trace to show sudden changes in the acoustic waveform decreases. For example, if a click lasts for only 5 ms, the window size is 20 ms, and the step between successive windows is 10 ms, how long would the click be in the RMS trace? In general, you shouldn't try to take duration measurements from RMS amplitude traces.

2.3.3 Fast Fourier transform (FFT)

The fast Fourier transform (FFT) is a digital signal processing method for calculating the Fourier transform (the spectrum) of a signal (Cooley et al., 1969). Recall from chapter 1 that Fourier analysis converts an acoustic waveform into a spectrum showing the sine wave components of the wave (see figures 1.5, 1.6, and 1.7 for an example). The FFT is a method of organizing the calculation of a Fourier transform that uses computer resources efficiently. The main practical concerns in using the FFT algorithm for Fourier analysis have to do with time resolution and frequency resolution. Naturally enough, there is a trade-off between them.

In the FFT algorithm, this trade-off is due to a connection between window size and frequency resolution. The frequency spectrum from 0 Hz to the Nyquist frequency (recall that the Nyquist frequency is half the sampling rate) is represented by a number of equally spaced points, and the number of points is determined by the number of samples in the waveform window (see the shaded box on "windowing"). Additionally, for computational ease (the "fast" part of FFT), the number of samples in the FFT waveform window must be a power of 2 (e.g. $2^7 = 128$, $2^8 = 256$, $2^9 = 512$, etc.).

Windowing

In DSP, "window" is both a noun and a verb. A waveform "window" is a segment or chunk of a waveform that has been "windowed."

Recall from chapter 1 that a transient signal has a flat spectrum (see figures 1.10 and 1.11). The relevance of this fact for FFT analysis is that when you select some arbitrary segment of a digital waveform, the first and last samples in the segment will almost always not be zero – and thus will be effectively transients. As a consequence, unless something is done, spectral analysis of arbitrary chunks of a digital waveform will erroneously include the spectrum of a transient signal. Windowing addresses this problem by modifying the amplitudes of the waveform segment so that samples nearer the edges are low in amplitude and samples in the middle of the segment are at full amplitude. Figure 2.10 illustrates the use of a window. Computer programs often offer several choices of window types. The two most common ones are "Hamming" and "rectangular." The Hamming window reduces the amplitudes of the samples near the edges of the waveform chunk, as illustrated in figure 2.10; whereas the rectangular window doesn't change the waveform samples at all. The Hamming window should be used in conjunction with FFT analysis, and rectangular windowing with all other types of analysis, including auto-correlation pitch tracking, RMS amplitude, and LPC analysis (section 2.3.5).

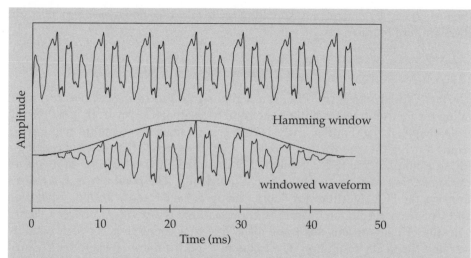

Figure 2.10 "Windowing" using a Hamming window. At the top is a waveform chunk. At the bottom a Hamming window is shown enveloping the "windowed" waveform.

Figure 2.11 No Hamming window is needed when the signal period exactly matches the analysis window duration. But when the waveform cycles do not exactly fit into the analysis window it is necessary to apply a Hamming (or similar) window before FFT analysis.

Here's an example of how windowing improves FFT analysis. Figure 2.11 shows three different FFT spectra. The first (the thin solid line) is the spectrum of a sine wave that fits exactly into the number of samples in the FFT window. That is, the window is exactly a multiple of the sinewave's period. Notice in this spectrum that there is one sharp peak at the frequency of the sinewave (a bit above 2000 Hz) and the rest of the spectrum has very low amplitude, at more than 200 dB down from the spectral peak. The spectrum drawn with the thick solid line is of a sinewave that has a very slightly different frequency, so that it doesn't exactly fit into the FFT analysis window. As you can see, this slight misfit between period duration and window length results in a spectrum with a smaller difference between the sinewave peak amplitude and the background "silence" amplitude. Finally, the third spectrum, drawn with a heavy dashed line, shows the result of applying a Hamming window to the misfit waveform. Now we have a spectrum which is much more similar to the case when the waveform fits exactly into the analysis window. For a complex signal like speech, windowing is essential in FFT analysis.

For example, with a sampling rate of 22 kHz and a window size of 1,024 samples – that is, a 46.5 ms chunk of the waveform (1,024 samples divided by 22,000 samples per second is 0.0465 seconds) – the interval between points in the computed spectrum is 21.48 Hz (22,000/1,024), giving estimates of the spectral amplitude at 21.48 Hz, 42.97 Hz, 64.45 Hz, etc. Spectral amplitudes for the intervening frequencies are not given by FFT, but if the interval between successive points in the spectrum is small, we may estimate the intervening points by interpolation (as is done when a computer program "connects the dots" in a graph of the spectrum).

Figure 2.12 shows a comparison of FFT spectra of a vowel sound calculated using a long analysis window (top spectrum) and a short analysis window (middle spectrum). There are two things to notice about these spectra. First, spectral details are better resolved when the analysis window is long. The more detailed spectrum derived from a long analysis window (1,024 samples) shows equally spaced, narrow peaks, which are called harmonics; while the spectrum derived from only 64 samples of the same waveform shows only the general spectral shape, and that shape is distorted because of the small number of points in the spectrum. Second, in order to achieve greater frequency resolution, an interval of 46.5 ms must be available for analysis. This is problematic, because there are many situations in speech analysis in which the spectrum changes over a very short time (5–10 ms), and either these temporal properties will not be captured in an FFT of a longer stretch, or, worse, the longer stretch will include a mixture of sounds, and thus the spectrum will include characteristics of discrete but adjacent sounds. Using a shorter analysis window avoids this problem – the 64-sample window is only 3 ms long when the sampling rate is 22 kHz – but spectral details are not captured, and the exact shape of the spectrum is very dependent on the location of the analysis window.

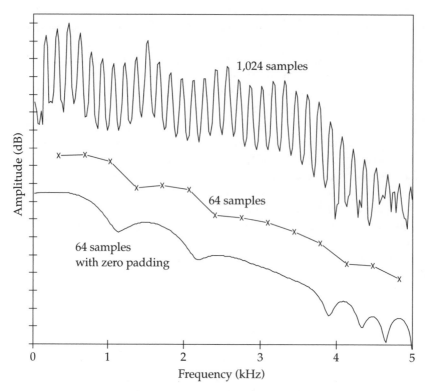

Figure 2.12   Window size and frequency resolution in FFT analysis. The top spectrum, labeled "1,024 samples," was produced using a 46 ms analysis window; hence it has high frequency resolution and low temporal resolution. The middle spectrum, labeled "64 samples," was produced using a 3 ms analysis window; hence it has high temporal resolution and low spectral resolution. Individual spectral estimates are marked with an x. The bottom spectrum, labeled "64 samples with zero padding," was produced by analyzing the same 3 ms waveform chunk in a zero-padded 46 ms analysis window. The interval between ticks on the vertical axis is 20 dB.

The bottom spectrum in figure 2.12 shows an interesting combination of long and short analysis windows. This spectrum is the result of analyzing 64 samples in a 1,024-point FFT, with the remaining 960 samples in the FFT window set at zero (this is called zero padding). That is, we increase the number of samples in the analysis window, and hence the frequency resolution of the spectrum, without increasing the number of signal samples analyzed. The result is similar to the 64-point spectrum in that only a broad outline of the spectral shape is captured, but the number of spectral amplitude points is large. Therefore, whereas the 64-point spectrum may be jagged, the zero-padded 64-point spectrum will show the broad spectral outline more accurately, because the frequency interval between spectral points is the same as in the 1,024-point spectrum.

Zero padding makes it possible to select an arbitrary number of samples for spectral analysis without having to worry about the frequency interval between spectral points; it thus makes it possible to select an arbitrary degree of temporal resolution and spectral smearing. Short windows are still very sensitive to their placement in the waveform, and long windows still tend to miss rapid spectral changes, but at least the number of samples in the computed spectrum is always adequate. This technique is used in digital spectrographs to control the degree of spectral smearing (the "width of the analysis filter") used in producing spectrograms of speech (more on this in section 2.3.6).

2.3.4   Digital filters

Digital audio signals can be easily edited and modified. Some editing operations are familiar from word processing. For example, waveform editors let you copy, cut, and paste waveform chunks. We can also modify the amplitude of a digital waveform by multiplying each sample with a scale factor – such as 0.5 to decrease the amplitude by one-half, or 2 to double the amplitude.

Getting a little more complicated, we can also make digital audio filters for low-pass, high-pass, and band-pass filtering. This chapter isn't going to go into digital filters in great depth (for that I recommend Lyons (1997)), but I do hope to get some basic concepts across so that you will know how to use digital filtering software and so that LPC analysis will be easier to understand.

We'll start with a very useful data smoothing technique called **moving average** smoothing. Of course, averaging a set of numbers replaces the range of possible values with one representative value. To smooth a time series of data (like an audio waveform) therefore it is common to replace each sample in the series with the average of nearby samples. An example of moving average smoothing is shown in figure 2.13.

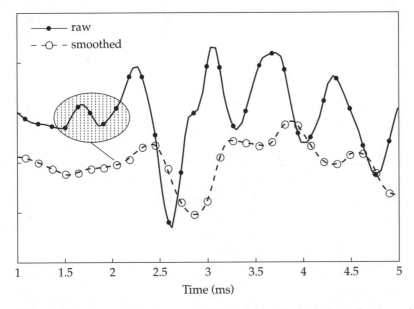

Figure 2.13 Data points from a raw audio waveform are averaged together to produce a moving average smoothed waveform. The smoothed waveform preserves the slow moving, low frequency, pattern of the raw waveform, but eliminates the jittery, fast moving, high frequency components such as the oscillation in the shaded oval.

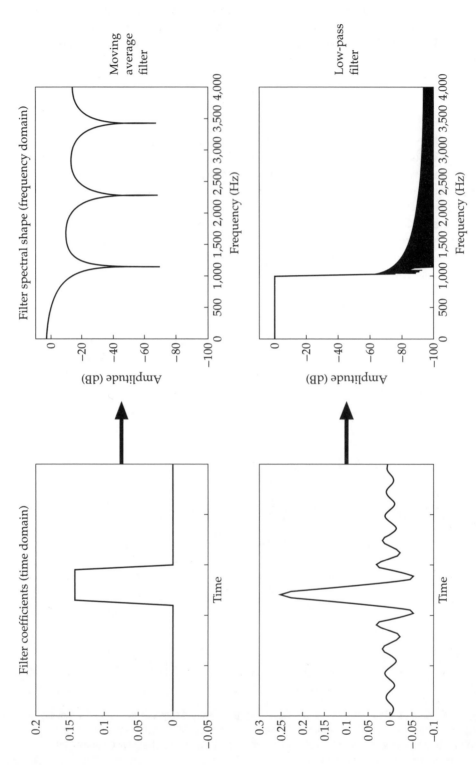

Figure 2.14 A comparison of the filter coefficients $h(k)$ and the resulting filter spectral shapes for the moving average low-pass filter and an ideal low-pass filter designed to have an extremely sharp transition between the pass band (below 1,000 Hz) and the stop band (above 1,000 Hz). One important difference between the filters is that the moving average filter has only seven coefficients, while the ideal low-pass filter has 579 coefficients.

The moving average smoothing technique is simply a form of low-pass filtering. The rapid changes from sample to sample in the raw waveform are removed (filtered out) from the smoothed waveform. To find the frequency response curve of the moving average filter we need to express the filter in a formula that isolates the **filter coefficients**. Let's say that the name of the smoothed waveform is $y(n)$ and that $x(n)$ is the raw waveform. In these abbreviations n refers to a time point, time n, and x and y are just arbitrary names that we give to the sampled digital waveforms. With these abbreviations we can then describe what we are doing to get the smoothed waveform from the raw one with equation (2.1).

$$y(n) = \frac{x(n-4) + x(n-3) + x(n-2) + x(n-1) + x(n-0)}{5} \tag{2.1}$$

The smoothed wave at time n ($y(n)$) is the average of the preceding five samples in the raw waveform ($x(n-4) \ldots x(n-0)$). We can simplify the equation so that it has a more generally useful form as in equation 2.2.

$$y(n) = \frac{1}{5}x(n-4) + \frac{1}{5}x(n-3) + \frac{1}{5}x(n-2) + \frac{1}{5}x(n-1) + \frac{1}{5}x(n-0)$$

$$= \sum_{k=0}^{M-1} \frac{1}{5}x(n-k) \tag{2.2}$$

$$= \sum_{k=0}^{M-1} h(k)x(n-k)$$

In equation (2.2) we distributed the 1/5 to each of the waveform samples, and then wrote the formula as a summation using a big sigma Σ to say that we are summing the multiplications for all values of k from 0 to $M-1$ where M is the number of samples being averaged (5 in this case). Finally, we replaced the constant 1/5 with a new variable $h(k)$ which in this example would be $h(0) = 1/5$, $h(1) = 1/5, \ldots, h(4) = 1/5$. This new sequence, $h(k)$, is the moving average filter – the values in this sequence are the **filter coefficients** and they determine the filter's frequency response characteristics. To determine the frequency profile of a filter all we have to do is perform an FFT analysis on the filter coefficients themselves (with zero padding). The graph in the upper right corner of figure 2.14 shows the results of doing this with the coefficients of a seven point moving average filter. One thing that is immediately obvious is that though the moving average smoother does provide some low-pass filtering, we could make a much more effective low-pass filter than this.

To make an ideal low-pass filter we can apply the Fourier transform in reverse, to go from the low-pass filter shape that we desire to the filter coefficients in $h(k)$ that will produce that degree of filtering when applied in equation (2.2). The process of "applying the Fourier transform in reverse" is called the Inverse Fourier Transform, or Inverse DFT. The filter coefficients that result from this process are shown in the bottom left graph in figure 2.14. The "ideal" filter shown in this figure has a very sharp transition at 1,000 Hz between the pass band and stop band. As the FFT of the filter coefficients (bottom right graph) shows, this low-pass filter will really eliminate all acoustic components above 1,000 Hz.

There are a number of "tricks of the trade" in designing digital filters. One of my favorites is that you can convert a low-pass filter into a high-pass filter by multiplying every other coefficient in $h(k)$ by −1, and more generally you can shift the center frequency of a low-pass filter (which has a center frequency of 0 Hz) by multiplying $h(k)$ with a digital sinewave of the desired center frequency. These things are all very interesting, but the key points to understand from this section are that (1) a digital filter is a sequence of coefficients $h(k)$ and that (2) we perform digital filtering by applying the filter like a moving average smoother as in equation (2.2). Incidentally, Lyons (1997) calls equation (2.2) "the infamous convolution equation," but if I had called it **convolution** you might have thought that things were getting too convoluted. Now you know.

2.3.5   Linear predictive coding (LPC)

In many instances in acoustic phonetics we are interested in broad spectral peaks, spanning several harmonic peaks, rather than the harmonics themselves. As suggested above, one way to see these global spectral patterns is to take an FFT of a small analysis window with zero padding. Another common technique for finding broad spectral peaks is called "linear predictive coding," or LPC.

LPC was invented by engineers working on low bit-rate communication systems. The original purpose was to save storage space in speech synthesis and recognition systems, and also for encrypted voice transmissions. LPC applies a physically sensible, if oversimplified, model of speech involving a sound source (vocal fold vibration) and a filter of several resonances. Because of this aspect, LPC analysis is a useful way of automatically determining the locations and widths of broad peaks in the speech spectrum. This section gives a rough outline of the relationship between auto-correlation pitch tracking and LPC analysis; in chapter 4 we will return to LPC analysis after discussing the acoustics of vocal tract resonance.

Recall from the discussion of auto-correlation pitch tracking above that one of the errors produced by the auto-correlation method is pitch-doubling. This happens when a sub-component of the pitch period is mistakenly identified as the pitch period. LPC analysis makes use of this tendency in auto-correlation analysis by limiting the auto-correlations to within the pitch period. In a sense, pitch-doubling is the desired result in LPC analysis.

It may be misleading, however, to tie pitch-doubling to LPC analysis, because this association implies that LPC will find only a waveform component that is double the F_0. This implication is wrong, because auto-correlation can determine the frequencies of an arbitrary number of waveform components in a complex wave.

Pre-emphasis

It is sometimes desirable in spectral analysis to increase the amplitudes of high-frequency components. In the analog speech spectrograph this is done with a soft high-pass filter (the "high-shaping" filter) that boosts the high-frequency components of the spectrum. In digital signal processing a high-frequency boost is added by "first-difference pre-emphasis."

To take the first difference of a digital waveform, you replace the waveform by the differences between adjacent samples ($y_n = x_n - x_{n-1}$). For instance, the waveform (0, 5, 9, 7, 3, –1, –5, –9, –6) is replaced by the successive differences ($5 - 0 = 5$, $9 - 5 = 4$, –2, –4, –4, –4, –4, 3). The spectral consequence of first differencing is surprising: the spectrum is tilted up by 6 decibels (dB) per doubling of frequency (octave). So, as the frequency doubles (one octave), the spectral amplitude becomes higher by 6 dB.

Many computer speech analysis packages allow you to specify pre-emphasis as a number between 0 and 1. If you specify 1, the result is first-difference pre-emphasis as described in the preceding paragraph. When the pre-emphasis value is less than 1 but greater than 0, the spectrum is tilted, but not as much as in first-difference pre-emphasis. This is done by taking differences between adjacent samples in the digital waveform as before, but multiplying the sample to be subtracted by the pre-emphasis value (p). The pre-emphasis formula is then: $y_n = x_n - px_{n-1}$. The pre-emphasis value, p, is usually set to a value between 0.90 and 0.98.

Figure 2.15 shows sub-components of a pitch period in the vowel schwa from the first vowel of the word *ahead*. Note that the figure shows only one pitch period, so both the "periods" indicated in the figure have smaller durations than the pitch period, hence higher frequencies. These frequencies are of broad spectral peaks such as those we saw in figure 2.13.

Recall that auto-correlation finds lag durations such that the waveform offset by the lag is a rough mirror image of itself. This is easiest to see for the sub-component identified as (a) in figure 2.15. A cyclic oscillation with a duration of 2 ms repeats approximately three times in the pitch period. Overlaid on this pattern – it might help to think of subtracting out oscillation (a) – is a faster-changing oscillation (b) that produces "ripples" on the peaks of the (a) component with a period duration of about 0.66 ms. The durations of the oscillations give their frequencies ($1/a = 500$ Hz, $1/b = 1{,}500$ HZ).

Figure 2.16 shows a Fourier spectrum of the waveform shown in figure 2.15. The arrows point to the frequencies derived from the auto-correlation LPC analysis illustrated in figure 2.15. Note that the spectrum is composed of harmonics of the fundamental frequency, and that the 500 Hz component that we identified by LPC analysis is between the third and fourth harmonics. This illustrates that LPC analysis finds the frequencies of broad spectral peaks in the spectrum, not merely the frequencies of the loudest harmonics in those broad peaks. In chapter 4,

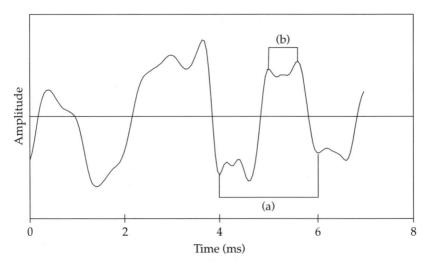

Figure 2.15 Frequency components in a pitch period, as identified by the auto-correlation method of LPC analysis. The figure shows one pitch period from the vowel schwa. The component labeled (a) is 2 ms long, and thus has a frequency of 500 Hz. The component labeled (b) is 0.66 ms long, and thus has a frequency of 1,500 Hz.

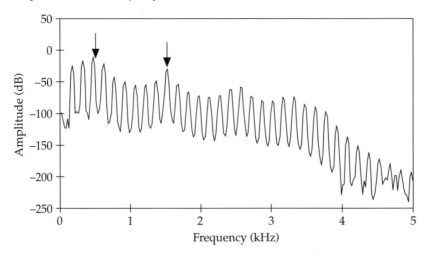

Figure 2.16 FFT spectrum of the waveform shown in figure 2.15. The arrows show the peak frequencies determined by auto-correlation LPC analysis.

after a discussion of the causes of spectral peaks in vowels, we will discuss LPC analysis further, including some practical suggestions for using computer implementations of LPC.

2.3.6 *Spectra and spectrograms*

One of the problems with analyzing vowels using power spectra is that time is not represented in the analysis. The power spectrum is more like a snapshot than a movie. We get a pretty accurate idea of the frequency components of a signal at a particular moment in time, but we have no idea what went on before or after the snapshot. Thus, for instance, we are likely to overlook the dynamic properties of diphthongs. The sound spectrograph offers a solution to this problem.

Here is one way to conceptualize what is going on in the sound spectrograph (note that the difference between the terms "spectrograph" and "spectrogram" is analogous to the difference between "telegraph" and "telegram"). Imagine that you take the spectrum of schwa shown in figure 2.16, and rather than represent the amplitude on a separate axis in the graph, you represent it by color. For instance, at 150 Hz there is an amplitude peak in the spectrum. Suppose that, rather than drawing this as a peak, we simply draw a dot on the frequency axis in yellow (a nice energetic color, to represent the fact that the amplitude at that frequency is high). Now suppose we adopt a color scheme such that any frequency component with an amplitude in the top tenth of the amplitude scale is indicated by yellow, any frequency component with an amplitude in the next tenth of the amplitude scale is indicated by red, and so on. We can now draw a spectrum, replacing the vertical axis with a color scheme, as a single line that changes color to show the approximate amplitudes of the components. But why go to the trouble of using a dimension like color to represent amplitude in the power spectrum? Because, by so doing, we can look at lots of spectra at once, to see spectral changes over time – the difference between a snapshot and a movie.

Here's how we take color-coded spectra and make a spectrogram. You make a color-coded spectrum, as described above. Then you move to a point a few milliseconds later in the waveform and make another color-coded spectrum, and put this spectrum with the first, building a stack of spectra. In order to line up the spectrogram with the acoustic waveform, we orient the spectra so that frequency is on the vertical axis, the first spectrum is on the left of the graph, and each successive spectrum is set just to the right of the one before it. Thus, time in a spectrogram is represented on the horizontal axis, frequency on the vertical axis, and amplitude is represented by color. For historical reasons, spectrograms usually encode amplitude using various shades of gray rather than color (with the peaks of the spectrum black, and the valleys white). The bottom half of figure 2.17 shows a spectrogram of a Cantonese speaker's pronunciation of the word [kaˈ] "chicken." A power spectrum and an LPC spectrum taken from a point late in the diphthong are shown in the top half. The vertical line in the spectrogram marks this point. Note the correspondence between the location of the vertical line in the power spectrum and the location of the short horizontal line in the spectrogram (both are located at 1.998 kHz). This illustrates that spectrograms and spectra show similar frequency information, but that spectrograms, like movies, show spectral changes over time, whereas spectra show only a single point in time. Note how the spectrogram shows that the frequency of the second broad spectral peak increases from the beginning of the vowel to the end. This type of change cannot be captured in a spectrum.

In spectrograms we usually want to smear the harmonics of the spectrum together, so that we can easily see broad spectral peaks in the spectrogram. In the

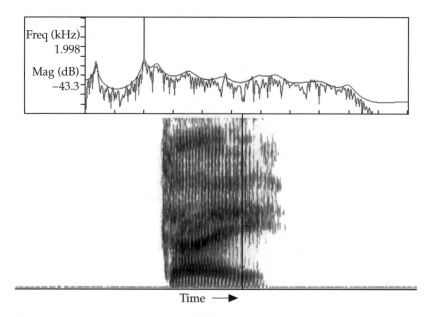

Figure 2.17   The bottom half of this figure shows a spectrogram of a Cantonese speaker's pronunciation of [kɑ¹] "chicken." Time is shown on the horizontal axis, and frequency (from 0 to 5 kHz) on the vertical axis. The top half shows a power spectrum and LPC analysis taken from a point (marked with the vertical line in the spectrogram) late in the diphthong. The vertical line in the spectrum marks the second broad spectral peak, which is marked in the spectrogram by a short horizontal line.

analog spectrograph (Potter et al., 1947; Joos, 1948) this was accomplished by analyzing the speech signal with a bank of band-pass filters that had relatively broad bandwidths. Each filter had a different center frequency, and responded only to energy within the band. For instance, if the fundamental frequency (F_0) is 150 Hz and the spectrograph filters have 300 Hz bandwidths, then the filters smear together adjacent harmonics, and the resulting spectrogram shows only the broad peaks of spectral energy, not the individual harmonics.

To produce digital spectrograms, we use FFT analysis to calculate the individual spectra, and we change the number of samples in the analysis window (with zero padding) to control the effective width of the analysis filter. An illustration of this was given in figure 2.12. For narrow-band spectrograms we use long analysis windows, giving us spectra which have high frequency resolution and low temporal resolution, whereas for wide-band spectrograms we use short analysis windows, giving us high temporal resolution (you can usually see individual voicing pulses, for example) and spectral smearing. In many ways, wide-band spectrograms are ideal for acoustic phonetics, because they capture temporal events very accurately while showing the general shape of the spectrum, and, as we will see in later chapters, we are often more interested in the general shape of the spectrum than in the fine spectral details.

Exercises

Sufficient jargon

Define the following terms: digital signal processing (DSP), continuous signals, discrete signals, analog devices, digital devices, sampling, quantization, analog-to-digital conversion, Nyquist frequency, sampling rate, aliasing, anti-aliasing filter, bit, quantization noise, signal-to-noise ratio, signal clipping, auto-correlation, waveform window, auto-correlation lag, pitch-halving, pitch-doubling, RMS amplitude, FFT, zero padding, windowing, pre-emphasis, LPC, spectrogram.

Short-answer questions

1 Use a ruler to "digitize" the waveform shown in figure 2.2. To do this, mark off equal intervals (in whatever units are convenient – inches, millimeters, etc.) on the time axis and on the amplitude axis, then complete the table below. Given that the figure shows 0.01 seconds, what is your sampling rate? How many amplitude steps are in your quantization scale?

time	amplitude
0	0

2 What is the Nyquist frequency for the following sampling rates: 16,000 Hz, 11.025 kHz, 20 Hz?

3 What should the cutoff frequency of an anti-aliasing filter be for the following sampling rates: 16,000 Hz, 11.025 kHz, 44 kHz?

4 How many amplitude steps can be represented if each sample is ten bits? What is the signal-to-noise ratio?

5 What lag duration in auto-correlation pitch tracking should (ideally) produce the highest correlation if the actual F_0 is 100 Hz, 200 Hz, 204 Hz?

6 What are the RMS amplitudes of sine waves that have the following peak amplitudes: 1; 75; 1,024?

7 What are the RMS amplitudes of sine waves that have the following peak-to-peak amplitudes: 2; 100; 1,834?

8 What is the size of the waveform window (in ms) if the sampling rate is 22 kHz and the window contains 512 samples?

9 How many samples are in a 20 ms window if the sampling rate is 22 kHz?

10 What is the interval between spectral points in an FFT spectrum if the sampling rate is 11 kHz and the window is 512 samples long?

11 What is the interval between spectral points in an FFT spectrum if the sampling rate is 22 kHz and the window is 5 ms long?

12 List the pre-emphasized amplitude values (using first-difference pre-emphasis) of the digitized waveform that you produced in answer to question 1.

CHAPTER 3

Basic Audition

The human auditory system is not a high-fidelity system. Amplitude is compressed; frequency is warped and smeared; and adjacent sounds may be smeared together. Because listeners experience auditory objects, not acoustic records like waveforms or spectrograms, it is useful to consider the basic properties of auditory perception as they relate to speech acoustics. This chapter starts with a brief discussion of the anatomy and function of the peripheral auditory system, then discusses two important differences between the acoustic and the auditory representation of sound, and concludes with a brief demonstration of the difference between acoustic analysis and auditory analysis using a computer simulation of auditory response. Later chapters will return to the topics introduced here as they relate to the perception of specific classes of speech sounds.

3.1 Anatomy of the peripheral auditory system

The peripheral auditory system (that part of the auditory system not in the brain) translates acoustic signals into neural signals; and in the course of the translation, it also performs amplitude compression and a kind of Fourier analysis of the signal.

Figure 3.1 illustrates the main anatomical features of the peripheral auditory system (see Pickles, 1988). Sound waves impinge upon the outer ear, and travel down the ear canal to the eardrum. The eardrum is a thin membrane of skin which is stretched like the head of a drum at the end of the ear canal. Like the membrane of a microphone, the eardrum moves in response to air pressure fluctuations.

outer ear

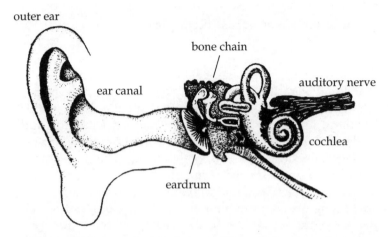

Figure 3.1 The main components of the human peripheral auditory system. Adapted from Brödel, 1946, fig. 1.

These movements are conducted by a chain of three tiny bones in the middle ear to the fluid-filled inner ear. There is a membrane (the basilar membrane) that runs down the middle of the conch-shaped inner ear (the cochlea). This membrane is thicker at one end than the other. The thin end, which is closest to the bone chain, responds to high-frequency components in the acoustic signal, while the thick end responds to low-frequency components. Each auditory nerve fiber innervates a particular section of the basilar membrane, and thus carries information about a specific frequency component in the acoustic signal. In this way, the inner ear performs a kind of Fourier analysis of the acoustic signal, breaking it down into separate frequency components.

3.2   The auditory sensation of loudness

The auditory system imposes a type of automatic volume control via amplitude compression, and as a result, it is responsive to a remarkable range of sound intensities (see Moore, 1982). For instance, the air pressure fluctuations produced by thunder are about 100,000 times larger than those produced by a whisper (see table 3.1).

Look at the values listed in the pressure column in the table. For most people, a typical conversation is not subjectively ten times louder than a quiet office, even though the magnitudes of their sound pressure fluctuations are. In general, subjective auditory impressions of loudness differences do not match sound pressure differences. The mismatch between differences in sound pressure and loudness has been noted for many years. For example, Stevens (1957) asked listeners to adjust the loudness of one sound until it was twice as loud as another or, in

How the inner ear is like a piano

For an example of what I mean by "responds to," consider the way in which piano strings respond to tones. Here's the experiment: go to your school's music department and find a practice room with a piano in it. Open the piano, so that you can see the strings. This works best with a grand or baby grand, but can be done with an upright. Now hold down the pedal that lifts the felt dampers from the strings and sing a steady note very loudly. Can you hear any of the strings vibrating after you stop singing? This experiment usually works better if you are a trained opera singer, but an enthusiastic novice can also produce the effect. Because the loudest sine wave components of the note you are singing match the natural resonant frequencies of one or more strings in the piano, the strings can be induced to vibrate sympathetically with the note you sing. The notion "natural resonant frequency" applies to the basilar membrane in the inner ear. The thick part naturally vibrates sympathetically with the low-frequency components of an incoming signal, while the thin part naturally vibrates sympathetically with the high-frequency components.

Table 3.1 A comparison of the typical maximum pressure fluctuations (given in both micro-Pascals (µPa), and decibels SPL) of some common sounds.

Typical experience	Pressure (µPa)	Decibel level (SPL)
Absolute threshold	20	0
Faint whisper	200	20
Quiet office	2,000	40
Conversation	20,000	60
City bus	200,000	80
Subway train	2,000,000	100
Loud thunder	20,000,000	120
Pain and damage	200,000,000	140

another task, until the first was half as loud as the second. Listeners' responses were converted into a scale of subjective loudness, the units of which are called "sones." The sone scale is plotted with open squares in figure 3.2. The left vertical axis of the graph shows listeners' judgments of relative loudness, scaled so that a sound about as loud as a quiet office (2,000 µPa) has a value of 1, a sound that is subjectively half as loud has a value of 0.5, and one that is twice as loud has a value of 2. As is clear in the figure, the relationship between sound pressure and

Figure 3.2   The nonlinearity of loudness perception is illustrated in this figure by plotting several sound pressure levels on both the sone scale and the dB scale.

loudness is not linear. For soft sounds, large changes in perceived loudness result from relatively small changes in sound pressure (the left end of the function is quite steep), while for loud sounds, relatively large pressure changes produce only small changes in perceived loudness. For example, if peak amplitude changes from 100,000 µPa to 200,000 µPa, the change in sones is greater than 2, but a change of the same pressure magnitude from 2,000,000 µPa to 2,100,000 µPa produces less than a 1 sone change in loudness.

Figure 3.2 also shows an older relative loudness scale that is named after Alexander Graham Bell. This unit of loudness, the bel, is too big for most purposes, and it is more common to use tenths of a bel, or decibels (abbreviated dB). This easily calculated scale is widely used in auditory phonetics and psychoacoustics, because it provides an approximation to the nonlinearity of human loudness sensation.

As the difference between dB SPL and dB SL implies, perceived loudness varies as a function of frequency. Figure 3.3 illustrates the relationship between subjective loudness and dB SPL. The curve in the figure represents the intensities of a set of tones that have the same subjective loudness as a 1,000 Hz tone presented at 60 dB SPL. The curve is like the settings of a graphic equalizer on a stereo. The lever on the left side of the equalizer controls the relative amplitude

Decibels

Although it is common to express the amplitude of a sound wave in terms of pressure, or, once we have converted acoustic energy into electrical energy, in volts, the decibel scale is a way of expressing sound amplitude that is better correlated with perceived loudness. On this scale the relative loudness of a sound is measured in terms of sound intensity (which is proportional to the square of the amplitude) on a logarithmic scale.

Consider a sound with average pressure amplitude x. Because sound intensity is proportional to the square of amplitude, the intensity of x relative to a reference sound with pressure amplitude r is x^2/r^2. A bel is the base 10 logarithm of this power ratio: $\log_{10}(x^2/r^2)$, and a decibel is 10 times this: $10 \log_{10}(x^2/r^2)$. This formula can be simplified to $20 \log_{10}(x/r) = dB$.

There are two common choices for the reference level r in dB measurements. One is 20 μPa, the typical absolute auditory threshold (lowest audible pressure fluctuation) of a 1,000 Hz tone. When this reference value is used, the values are labeled dB SPL (for Sound Pressure Level). The other common choice for the reference level has different reference pressure levels for each frequency. In this method, rather than use the absolute threshold for a 1,000 Hz tone as the reference for all frequencies, the loudness of a tone is measured relative to the typical absolute threshold level for a tone at that frequency. When this method is used, the values are labeled dB SL (for Sensation Level).

In speech analysis programs, amplitude may be expressed in dB relative to the largest amplitude value that can be taken by a sample in the digital speech waveform, in which case the amplitude values are negative numbers; or it may be expressed in dB relative to the smallest amplitude value that can be represented in the digital speech waveform, in which case the amplitude values are positive numbers. These choices for the reference level in the dB calculation are used when it is not crucial to know the absolute dB SPL value of the signal. For instance, calibration is not needed for comparative RMS or spectral amplitude measurements.

of the lowest-frequency components in the music, while the lever on the right side controls the relative amplitude of the highest frequencies. This "equal loudness" contour shows that you have to amplify the lowest and highest frequencies if you want them to sound as loud as the middle frequencies (whether this sounds good is another issue). So, as the figure shows, the auditory system is most sensitive to sounds that have frequencies between 2 and 5 kHz. Note also that sensitivity drops off quickly above 10 kHz. This was part of my motivation in chapter 2 for choosing a sampling rate of 22 kHz (11 kHz Nyquist frequency) for acoustic/phonetic analysis.

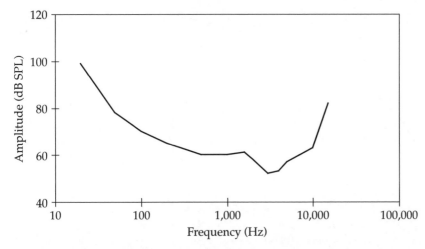

Figure 3.3   Equal loudness curve for pure tones presented over a loudspeaker. The line connects tones that have the same subjective loudness as a 1,000 Hz tone presented at 60 dB SPL.

3.3   Frequency response of the auditory system

As discussed in section 3.1, the auditory system performs a running Fourier analysis of incoming sounds. However, this physiological frequency analysis is not the same as the mathematical Fourier decomposition of signals. The main difference is that the auditory system's frequency response is not linear. Just as a change of 1,000 μPa in a soft sound is not perceptually equivalent to a similar change in a loud sound, so a change from 500 to 1,000 Hz is not perceptually equivalent to a change from 5,000 to 5,500 Hz. This is illustrated in figure 3.4, which shows the relationship between an auditory frequency scale called the Bark scale (Zwicker, 1961; Schroeder et al., 1979), and acoustic frequency in kHz. Zwicker (1975) showed that the Bark scale is proportional to a scale of perceived pitch (the Mel scale) and to distance along the basilar membrane. A tone with a frequency of 500 Hz has an auditory frequency of 4.9 Bark, while a tone of 1,000 Hz is 8.5 Bark, a difference of 3.6 Bark. On the other hand, a tone of 5,000 Hz has an auditory frequency of 19.2 Bark, while one of 5,500 Hz has an auditory frequency of 19.8 Bark, a difference of only 0.6 Bark. The line shown in figure 3.4 represents the fact that the auditory system is more sensitive to frequency changes at the low end of the audible frequency range than at the high end.

This nonlinearity in the sensation of frequency is related to the fact that the listener's experience of the pitch of periodic sounds and of the timbre of complex sounds is largely shaped by the physical structure of the basilar membrane. Figure 3.5 illustrates the relationship between frequency and location along the basilar membrane. As mentioned earlier, the basilar membrane is thin at its base and thick at its apex; as a result, the base of the basilar membrane responds to high-frequency sounds, and the apex to low-frequency sounds. As figure 3.5 shows, a relatively large portion of the basilar membrane responds to sounds

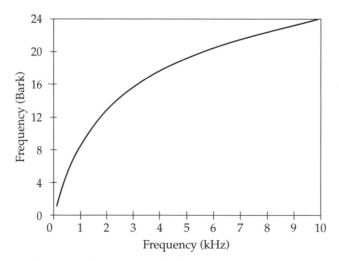

Figure 3.4 Comparison of an auditory frequency scale (the Bark scale) and an acoustic frequency scale (in kHz), showing that the auditory system is more sensitive to small changes in frequency at the low end of the audible range.

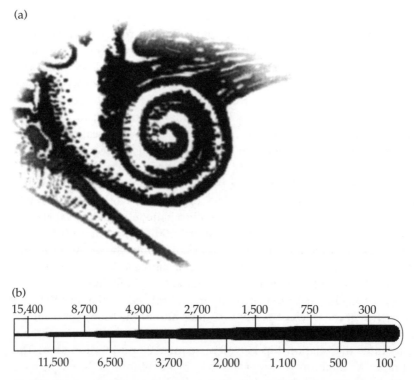

Figure 3.5 (a) shows the inner ear, (b) the approximate locations of sensitivity to representative frequencies along the basilar membrane when the inner ear is "uncoiled." See figure 3.1 to locate the inner ear in relation to other parts of the peripheral auditory system.

below 1,000 Hz, whereas only a small portion responds to sounds between 12,000 and 13,000 Hz, for example. Therefore, small changes in frequency below 1,000 Hz are more easily detected than are small changes in frequency above 12,000 Hz. The relationship between auditory frequency and acoustic frequency shown in figure 3.4 is due to the structure of the basilar membrane in the inner ear.

3.4   Auditory representations

In practical terms what all this means is that when we calculate an acoustic power spectrum of a speech sound, the frequency and loudness scales of the analyzing device (for instance, a computer or a spectrograph) are not the same as the auditory system's frequency and loudness scales. Consequently, acoustic analyses of speech sounds may not match the listener's experience. The resulting mismatch is especially dramatic for sounds like some stop release bursts and fricatives that have a lot of high-frequency energy. One way to avoid this mismatch between acoustic analysis and the listener's experience is to implement a functional model of the auditory system. Some examples of the use of auditory models in speech analysis are Liljencrants and Lindblom (1972), Bladon and Lindblom (1981), Johnson (1989), Lyons (1982), Patterson (1976), Moore and Glasberg (1983), and Seneff (1988). Figure 3.6 shows the difference between the auditory and

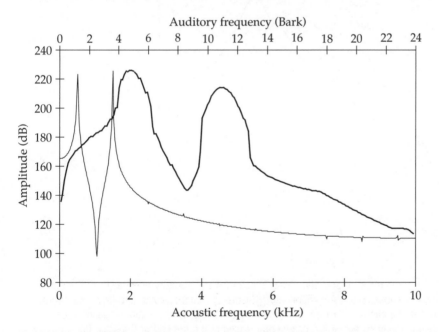

Figure 3.6   A comparison of acoustic (light line) and auditory (heavy line) spectra of a complex wave composed of sine waves at 500 at 1,500 Hz. Both spectra extend from 0 to 10 kHz, although on different frequency scales. The auditory spectrum was calculated from the acoustic spectrum using the model described in Johnson (1989).

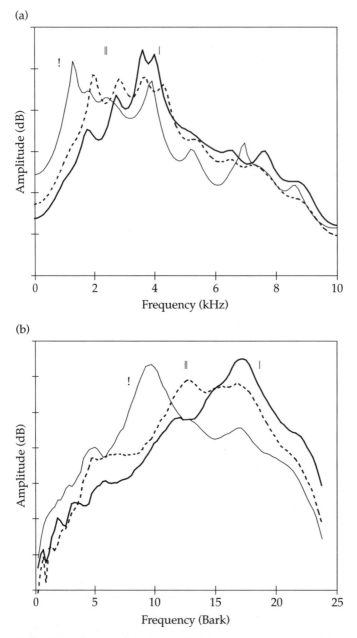

Figure 3.7 A comparison of acoustic power spectra (a) and auditory spectra (b) of three click release bursts in Xhosa. The IPA symbols are [|] dental, [!] post-alveolar, and [||] lateral. In the acoustic spectra the clicks differ from each other below 6 kHz. In the auditory spectra the nondistinctive frequencies above 6 kHz are compressed at the top end of the scale (above) 20 Bark (after Johnson, 1992). The interval between ticks on the vertical axes is 10 dB.

acoustic spectra of a complex wave composed of a 500 Hz and a 1,500 Hz sine wave component. The vertical axis is amplitude in dB, and the horizontal axis shows frequency in Hz, marked on the bottom of the graph, and Bark, marked on the top of the graph. I made this auditory spectrum, and others shown in later figures, with a computer program (Johnson, 1989) that mimics the frequency response characteristics shown in figure 3.4 and the equal loudness contour shown in figure 3.3. Notice that because the acoustic and auditory frequency scales are different, the peaks are located at different places in the two representations, even though both spectra cover the frequency range from 0 to 10,000 Hz. Almost half of the auditory frequency scale covers frequencies below 1,500 Hz, while this same range covers less than two-tenths of the acoustic display. So, low-frequency components tend to dominate the auditory spectrum. Notice too that in the auditory spectrum there is some frequency smearing that causes the peak at 11 Bark (1,500 Hz) to be somewhat broader than that at 5 Bark (500 Hz). This spectral-smearing effect increases as frequency increases.

Figure 3.7 shows an example of the difference between acoustic and auditory spectra of speech. The acoustic spectra of the release bursts of the clicks in Xhosa are shown in (a), while (b) shows the corresponding auditory spectra. Like figure 3.6, this figure shows several differences between acoustic and auditory spectra. First, the region between 6 and 10 kHz (20–4 Z in the auditory spectra), in which the clicks do not differ very much, is not very prominent in the auditory spectra. In the acoustic spectra this insignificant portion takes up two-fifths of the frequency scale, while it takes up only one-fifth of the auditory frequency scale. This serves to visually, and presumably auditory, enhance the differences between the spectra. Second, the auditory spectra show many fewer local peaks than do the acoustic spectra. In this regard it should be noted that the acoustic spectra shown in figure 3.7 were calculated using LPC analysis to smooth them; the FFT spectra which were input to the auditory model were much more complicated than these smooth LPC spectra. The smoothing evident in the auditory spectra on the other hand is due to the increased bandwidths of the auditory filters at high frequencies.

Auditory models are interesting, because they offer a way of looking at the speech signal from the point of view of the listener. The usefulness of auditory models in phonetics depends on the accuracy of the particular simulation of the peripheral auditory system. Therefore, the illustrations in this book were produced by models that implement only well-known, and extensively studied, nonlinearities in auditory loudness and frequency response, and avoid areas of knowledge that are less well understood for complicated signals like speech.

These rather conservative auditory representations suggest that acoustic analyses give only a rough approximation to the auditory representations that listeners use in identifying speech sounds.

Recall from chapter 2 that digital spectrograms are produced by encoding spectral amplitude in a series of FFT spectra as shades of gray in the spectrogram. This same method of presentation can also be used to produce auditory spectrograms from sequences of auditory spectra. Figure 3.8 shows an acoustic

Figure 3.8 Comparison of a normal acoustic spectrogram (top), and an auditory spectrogram, or cochleagram (bottom), of the Cantonese word [kaɪ] "chicken." The cochleagram was produced by Lyons's (1982) cochlear model.

spectrogram and an auditory spectrogram of the Cantonese word [kɑ¹] "chicken" (see figure 2.17). To produce this figure, I used a publicly available auditory model (Lyons's cochlear model (Lyons, 1982; Slaney, 1988), which can be found at: ftp://ftp.ling.ohio-state.edu/pub/phonetics/ear). The auditory spectrogram, which is also called a "cochleagram," combines features of auditory spectra and spectrograms. As in a spectrogram, the simulated auditory response is represented with spectral amplitude plotted as shades of gray, with time on the horizontal axis and frequency on the vertical axis. Note that although the same frequency range (0–11 kHz) is covered in both displays, the movements of the lowest concentrations of spectral energy in the vowel are much more visually pronounced in the cochleagram because of the auditory frequency scale. The following chapters will make use of cochleagrams to explore the auditory properties of various classes of speech sounds.

Exercises

Sufficient jargon

Define the following terms: peripheral auditory system, eardrum, middle ear, inner ear, cochlea, basilar membrane, natural resonant frequency, sone, decibel, dB SPL, dB SL, equal loudness contour, Bark scale, auditory model, auditory spectrum, cochleagram.

Short-answer questions

1   Refering to figure 3.2, what is the sound pressure level (in μPa) of a sound that is 6 sones loud? What is the sound pressure level of a sound that is subjectively twice as loud as a 6 sone sound?
2   Refering to figure 3.3, which is subjectively louder: a 100 Hz sine wave at 65 dB SPL or a 1 000 Hz sine wave at 60 dB SPL, a 15,000 Hz sine wave at 80 dB SPL or a 2,000 Hz sine wave at 70 dB SPL, a 500 Hz sine wave at 60 dB SL or a 9,000 Hz sine wave at 60 dB SL?
3   Refering to figure 3.4, what is the auditory frequency in Bark of each of the following sine waves: 7 kHz, 8 kHz, 1 kHz, 2 kHz? Which is the bigger difference in auditory frequency, 7 kHz to 8 kHz or 1 kHz to 2 kHz?
4   Plot the relationship between distance traveled by sounds and their subjective loudnesses. Here is a set of sounds that you could use in this exercise: a card (like a business card, or a credit card) tapping on a table or car hood, a pen tapping on a table, a ruler tapping on a table, and a coffee mug tapping on a table. The idea is that the sounds will cover a managable range of loudness. You can use other sounds if you want, but choose minimally four things and choose things that are similar in time (like tapping).
    Do this exercise with a partner. First, both of you should independently rate the loudness of the sounds by filling in the following blanks with numbers (use fractions if you want).

(a)   The pen is————times louder than the card.
(b)   The ruler is————times louder than the pen.
(c)   The mug is————times louder than the ruler.

You can make a subjective loudness scale by setting the loudness of the card to 1, then set the loudness of the pen to 1 times the number given in (a), and the loudness of the ruler as the loudness of the pen times the number given in (b), and the loudness of the mug as the loudness of the ruler times the number given in (c). How different is your scale from your partner's scale?

Now measure loudness a different way. Find a hallway or an open yard or field. As one person makes the noise, the other should walk away and stop walking when he/she can no longer hear the noise. The noise-maker should count the number of steps the listener takes and mark this down for the sound. Repeat this for each sound and for both partners. How different is your scale from your partner's scale?

How do these two loudness scales compare with each other? Try plotting them the way sones are plotted against pressure in figure 3.2. Is the relationship linear? non-linear? Is one scale more like the sones scale and one more like the sound pressure scale? How would you convert the distance scale into sound pressure?

CHAPTER 4

Speech Perception

The perceptual representation of speech is different from its auditory representation. Acoustically, speech sounds are sound waves that are produced by vocal tracts in motion. Auditorily, they are shaped by the nonlinearities of the auditory system. Perceptually, speech sounds are no longer even limited to audition – the visual image of the talker plays a role in perception – and perception takes place in the context of a lifetime of experience with language.

The acoustic descriptions which form the primary topic of this book open the way to some very important insights about language. But as we saw in the previous chapter, the ear is not a high fidelity transmission system. The mental representation of speech has been warped by the auditory system. So, we will pay attention to the auditory mapping of speech. But now, in this chapter, we will consider the ways that the brain codes speech. This chapter has two main points. First, I hope to convince you that it is relatively easy to study speech perception; so easy, in fact, that you can start studying speech perception right away. Second, I hope to show that the perceptual representations of speech are built from auditory input **plus** other information.

4.1 A speech perception experiment

The study of speech perception starts with confusion. Maybe all scientific endeavors do – why else conduct research? But speech perception research literally starts with confusion because in the typical experiment we play sounds to people and ask them what they heard and hope that they will sometimes get the wrong answer. We analyze the pattern of wrong answers, the confusions, to determine the structure of the "perceptual space" used by listeners.

The next few pages will walk you through the steps of a speech perception experiment. Here's a preview of the steps:

1   Decide what to study – select examples to use in an experiment
2   Record multiple repetitions of each test syllable (call these tokens)
3   Digitize the tokens and make a separate sound file for each one
4   Add noise to the tokens
5   Make an answer sheet
6   Put the tokens in random order
7   Play the tokens in random order onto tape
8   Play the test tape to listeners
9   Tabulate the responses into a confusion matrix

Experimental paradigms

There is no end to how clever people can be when it comes to devising listening experiments. Things can get really complicated as we attempt to control our listeners' thought patterns during the course of the experiment. We don't want them to guess the purpose of the experiment so we embed the "test trials" in a large number of "filler trials." Or, we try to give very detailed specific instructions so that listeners will approach the task in a particular way. I have found that listeners tend to be influenced by the structure of the experiment and by the structure of the stimuli much more than by the instructions that you give (see, for example, the failed instruction manipulations in Johnson, Flemming and Wright, 1993). In speech perception experiments this dependence on stimuli and experiment design can be so complete that the listener can know exactly what the experiment is for, what the expected results are, and even have lots of practice listening to the stimuli and still produce results that are practically the same as listeners who have no idea about these things and don't care either. I find that my own listening responses are often very much like those of "naive" subjects.

When it comes to describing the experimental procedures that you might use in a speech perception experiment the options listed below may be helpful. The experiment that we are describing in this section uses naturally produced stimuli (just a recording of someone saying nonsense syllables) that have been modified by adding white noise. The listener's task is to identify the initial phoneme of each test syllable. In a discrimination task we might ask listeners to hear a pair of stimuli and tell whether the two presented syllables are the same or different. Or in a matching task we might present three stimuli in a row and ask if the middle one is more like the first one or the last one. In most experiments we are simply interested in the response choices that people make, but sometimes we also measure how long it takes to make that choice. Finally, experiments can be characterized according to the group of people who

Stimuli: Measure:
  natural   response choice
  modified natural   response time
  synthesized
Listener's task: Subject population:
  identification   hearing ability
  discrimination   talker's language
  matching   listener's language

participate as listeners – whether we are studying hearing deficits or cross-linguistic perception.

The first step is to decide what to study. I'm interested in why English [ð] is sometimes pronounced as [z] and sometimes as [d] by speakers who learn English as a second (or third, or fourth) language. I notice this especially with the function words "this" and "that" [zɪs] and [zæt] or [dɪs] and [dæt]. This variation also occurs across some dialects of English. I'm also personally interested in a similar phenomenon with [θ] and [f] – as for example when my niece Erin decided that my name is [kif].

So, that's the general context for a study of speech sounds. In particular though, let's hypothesize that perceptual confusability underlies patterns of substitution involving fricatives in English. This hypothesis predicts that the consonants that substitute for each other (e.g. [ð]/[z]/[d] and [θ]/[f]) are perceptually similar to each other. So now we need to do an experiment to test this hypothesis.

Here's how it works. First, we record someone saying some test syllables. These can be monosyllabic nonsense words. To start with we can record syllables with initial fricative sounds (and the stop [d] – to test the "dis" and "dat" hypothesis). For example, let's choose [fɑ], [vɑ], [sɑ], [zɑ], [θɑ], [ðɑ], and [dɑ]. We'll have our speaker pronounce each test syllable ten times so that we don't end up relying on one particular, possibly weird, pronunciation of the test syllable. Then we digitize them into a computer and make separate sound files (e.g. fa1.wav, va1.wav, sa1.wav, za1.wav, tha1.wav, dha1.wav, and da1.wav, fa2.wav ...) so that we end up with 70 sound files – seven test syllables with ten renditions of each.

Now we add some noise to copies of the sound files so that we have fa1_noise.wav, sa1_noise.wav, etc. It is pretty easy to add noise to a sound file because many waveform editors have an editing function called "add noise." You can just play around with the add noise function and find a level so that the noise is subjectively about as loud as the speech signal. When the noise has the same loudness as the speech the signal to noise ratio (SNR) will be at about 0 dB. If you want to be more accurate about signal to noise ratio, you can measure loudness in earphones with a loudness level meter (available at your local stereo

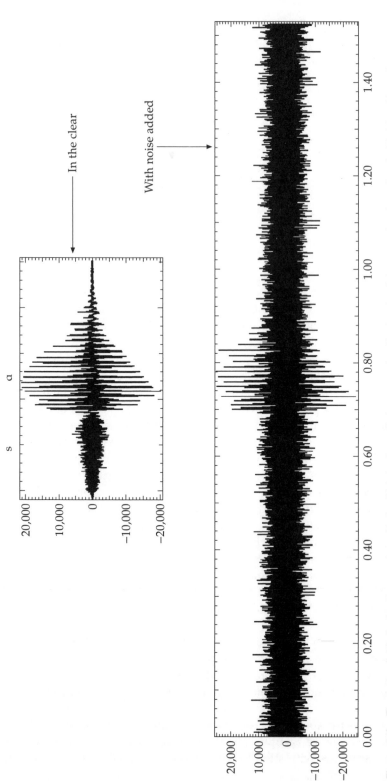

Figure 4.1 The test syllable [sɑ] with no noise added, which is also called presentation "in the clear" (top waveform), and embedded in white noise at a signal to noise ratio of 0 dB (bottom waveform). This figure illustrates that SNR is based on sound power and not on peak amplitude.

shop). By the way, before adding noise you'll want to add a short interval of silence before and after the test syllable so that the test syllable will be embedded in noise. A half a second (500 ms) before and after the test syllable is enough. Figure 4.1 shows one of the test syllables in the clear and with noise added.

Ok, so we have test syllables that differ by only their initial consonant, and we have embedded these in noise. Now it is time to present them to listeners, right? Well, not quite. First, let's make a test tape that has all of the test syllables on it. We'll want to present the test syllables in random order so that listeners have to listen closely to each token. You can do this pretty easily by assigning a random number to each of the 70 test syllables (using a random number function in a spreadsheet program, or by using a random number table from the back of a statistics text book) and then sorting the syllables by their random numbers from smallest random number to largest, or the other way if you want. To make the test "tape" you could construct a long computer sound file that contains the test tokens in random order and silent intervals inserted between the sound files. Then you could just play the sound file from the computer without bothering with a tape recorder. Or you could make the tape by playing sound files out to a tape recorder. This involves a procedure with the following steps – press record, play a file, let the recorder run while you count to three, pause the recorder, load the next file, release the pause, play the file, count to three, pause the tape, and so on. Tedious but low tech. In either case (tape or computer), be sure to leave enough time to complete the task for each token, and leave longer gaps at regular intervals, for example every ten tokens, so that people won't get lost on the answer sheet.

So, of course, we will need an answer sheet for our listeners to use. Here are the first four lines that I would use for the fricative test for American English listeners:

1   fa va tha dha sa za da
2   fa va tha dha sa za da
3   fa va tha dha sa za da
4   fa va tha dha sa za da

The listener's instruction is to listen to the first token and circle the correct answer in row 1 of the answer sheet, then listen to the second token and circle the correct answer in row 2, and so on.

There's an obvious problem isn't there? The test syllables include two sounds that aren't distinguished in English orthography [θ] and [ð]. If I am going to go through with this test with American English listeners I would have to try to teach them about these two sounds, that they will be written with "th" and "dh" on the answer sheet, and practice with them until they get it. We'll come back to this problem later in the chapter.

Let's say that we present each one of our 70 test syllables to ten listeners. This would result in 700 identification responses. To analyze these responses we will tabulate them in a **confusion matrix.** Each row in the matrix corresponds to one

Table 4.1 Fricative (and [d]) confusions from Miller and Nicely (1955).

	"f"	"v"	"th"	"dh"	"s"	"z"	"d"	Other	Total
[f]	199	0	46	1	4	0	0	14	264
[v]	3	177	1	29	0	4	0	22	236
[θ]	85	2	114	0	10	0	0	21	232
[ð]	0	64	0	105	0	18	0	17	204
[s]	5	0	38	0	170	0	0	15	228
[z]	0	4	0	22	0	132	17	49	224
[d]	0	0	0	4	0	8	189	59	260

of the test syllables (collapsing across all ten tokens of that syllable) and each column in the matrix corresponds to one of the responses available to listeners.

I didn't actually conduct this experiment, but table 4.1 shows the confusion matrix for the 0 dB SNR condition in a larger study conducted by George Miller and Patricia Nicely in 1955. Yep, these data are old, but they're good. Looking at the first row of the confusion matrix we see that [f] was presented 264 times and correctly identified as "f" 199 times and as "th" 46 times. Note that Miller and Nicely have more data for some sounds than for others.

That's it! We designed and constructed a speech perception experiment and now we have the data all nicely laid out in a confusion matrix. We can even get some pretty quick answers out of the confusion matrix. For example, why is it that "Keith" is sometimes pronounced "Keif" by children? Well, according to Miller and Nicely's data, [θ] was called "f" 85 times out of 232 – it was confused with "f" more often than with any other speech sound tested. Cool. But it isn't clear that these data tell us anything at all about the realizations of "this" and "that." To address that question we need to find a way to map the perceptual "space" that underlies the confusions we observe in our experiment. It is to this mapping problem we now turn.

4.2 Maps from distances

So, we're trying to pull information out of a confusion matrix to get a picture of the perceptual system that caused the confusions. The strategy that we will use takes a list of distances and reconstructs them as a map. Consider for example the list of distances below for cities in Ohio.

Columbus to Cincinnati, 107 miles
Columbus to Cleveland, 142 miles
Cincinnati to Cleveland, 249 miles

From these distances we can put these cities on a straight line as in figure 4.2(a), with Columbus located between Cleveland and Cincinnati. A line works to describe

Figure 4.2 (a) A one dimensional map showing the relative locations of three cities in Ohio. (b) A two dimensional map showing the relative locations of three Dutch cities. The gray arcs illustrate how we place Nijmegen using the procedure of triangulation.

these distances because the distance from Cincinnati to Cleveland is simply the sum of the other two distances (107 + 142 = 249). Here's an example that requires a two dimensional plane.

Amsterdam to Groningen, 178 km
Amsterdam to Nijmegen, 120 km
Groningen to Nijmegen, 187 km

The two-dimensional map that plots the distances between these cities in The Netherlands is shown in figure 4.2(b). To produce this figure I put Amsterdam and Groningen on a line and called the distance between them 178 km. Then I drew an arc 120 km from Amsterdam, knowing that Nijmegen has to be somewhere on this arc. Then I drew an arc 187 km from Groningen, knowing that Nijmegen also has to be somewhere on this arc. So, Nijmegen has to be at the intersection of the two arcs – 120 km from Amsterdam and 187 km from Groningen. This method of locating a third point based on its distance from two known points is called triangulation. The triangle shown in figure 4.2(b) is an

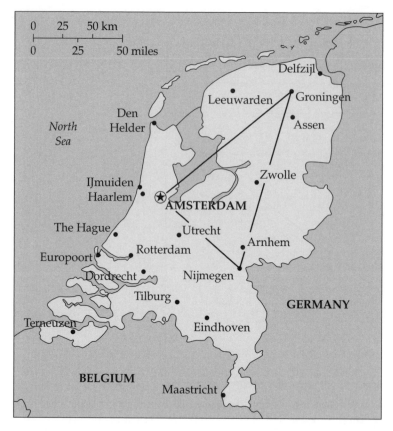

Figure 4.3 A map of the Netherlands showing the orientation of the Amsterdam–Groningen–Nijmegen triangle derived in figure 4.2(b).

accurate depiction of the relative locations of these three cities as you can see in the map in figure 4.3.

You might be thinking to yourself, "Well, this is all very nice, but what does it have to do with speech perception?" Good question. It turns out that we can compute perceptual distances from a confusion matrix. And by using an extension of triangulation called multi-dimensional scaling, we can produce a perceptual map from a confusion matrix.

4.3 The perceptual map of fricatives

In this section we will use multidimensional scaling to map the perceptual space that caused the confusion pattern in table 4.1.

The first step in this analysis process is to convert confusions into distances. We believe that this is a reasonable thing to try to do because we assume that when things are close to each other in perceptual space they will get confused with each other in the identification task. So the errors in the matrix in table 4.1 tell us what gets confused with what. Notice, for example, that the voiced consonants [v], [ð], [z] and [d] are very rarely confused with the voiceless consonants [f], [θ] and [s]. This suggests that voiced consonants are close to each other in perceptual space while voiceless consonants occupy some other region. Generalized statements like this are all well and good, but we need to compute some specific estimates of perceptual distance from the confusion matrix.

Here's one way to do it (I'm using the method suggested by the mathematical psychologist Roger Shepard in his important 1972 paper "Psychological representation of speech sounds"). There are two steps. First, calculate similarity and then from the similarities we can derive distances.

Similarity is easy. The number of times that you think [f] sounds like "θ" is a reflection of the similarity of "f" and "θ" in your perceptual space. Also, "f"–"θ" similarity is reflected by the number of times you say that [θ] sounds like "f", so we will combine these two cells in the confusion matrix – [f] heard as "θ" and [θ] heard as "f." Actually, since there may be a different number of [f] and [θ] tokens presented, we will take proportions rather than raw counts.

Notice that for any two items in the matrix we have a submatrix of four cells: (a) is the submatrix of response proportions for the "f"/"θ" contrast from Miller and Nicely's data. Note for example that the value 0.75 in this table is the proportion of [f] tokens that were recognized as "f" (199/264 = 0.754). Listed with the submatrix are two abstractions from it.

(a)

	"f"	"θ"
[f]	0.75	0.17
[θ]	0.37	0.49

(b)

	"f"	"f"
[f]	p_{ff}	$p_{f\theta}$
[θ]	$p_{\theta f}$	$p_{\theta\theta}$

(c)

	"i"	"j"
[i]	p_{ii}	p_{ij}
[j]	p_{ji}	p_{jj}

The variables in submatrix (b) code the proportions so that "p" stands for proportion, the first subscript letter stands for the row label and the second subscript letter stands for the column label. So $p_{\theta f}$ is a variable that refers to the proportion of times that [θ] tokens were called "f". In these data $p_{\theta f}$ is equal to 0.37. Submatrix (c) abstracts this a little further to say that for any two sounds i and j, we have a submatrix with confusions (subscripts don't match) and correct answers (subscripts match).

Asymmetry in confusion matrices

Is there some deep significance in the fact that [θ] is called "f" more often than [f] is called "th"? It may be that listeners had a bias against calling things "th" – perhaps because it was confusing to have to distinguish between "th" and "dh" on the answer sheet. This would seem to be the case in table 4.1 because there are many more "f" responses than "th" responses overall. However, the relative infrequency of "s" responses suggests that we may not want to rely too heavily on a response bias explanation because the "s" to [s] mapping is common and unambiguous in English. Shepard's method for calculating similarity from a confusion matrix assumes that $p_{f\theta}$ and $p_{\theta f}$ are two imperfect measures of the same thing – the confusability of "f" and "θ." These two estimates are thus combined to form one estimate of "f"–"θ" similarity. This is not to deny that there might be something interesting to look at in the asymmetry, but only that for the purpose of making perceptual maps the sources of asymmetry in the confusion matrix are ignored.

Here is Shepard's method for calculating similarity from a confusion matrix. We take the confusions between the two sounds and scale them by the correct responses. In math, that's:

$$S_{ij} = \frac{p_{ij} + p_{ji}}{p_{ii} + p_{jj}} \tag{4.1}$$

In this formula, S_{ij} is the similarity between category i and category j. In the case of "f" and "θ" in Miller and Nicely's data (table 4.1) the calculation is:

$$S_{ij} = 0.43 = \frac{0.17 + 0.37}{0.75 + 0.49}$$

I should say that regarding this formula Shepard simply says that it "has been found serviceable." Sometimes you can get about the same results by simply taking the average of the two confusion proportions p_{ij} and p_{ji} as your measure of similarity, but Shepard's formula does a better job with a confusion matrix in which one category has confusions concentrated between two particular responses, while another category has confusions fairly widely distributed among possible responses – as might happen, for example, when there is a bias against using one particular response alternative.

OK, so that's how to get a similarity estimate from a confusion matrix. To get perceptual distance from similarity you simply take the negative of the natural log of the similarity. Ahhem, in math that is:

$$d_{ij} = -\ln(S_{ij}) \tag{4.2}$$

This is based on Shepard's Law, which states that the relationship between perceptual distance and similarity is exponential. There may be a deep truth about mental processing in this law – it comes up in all sorts of unrelated contexts (Shannon and Weaver, 1949; Parzen, 1962), but that's a different topic.

Table 4.2 Similarities among American English fricatives (and [d]), based on the 0 dB SNR confusion matrix from Miller and Nicely (1955).

	"f"	"v"	"th"	"dh"	"s"	"z"	"d"
[f]	1.0						
[v]	.008	1.0					
[θ]	.434	.010	1.0				
[ð]	.003	.345	.000	1.0			
[s]	.025	.000	.170	.000	1.0		
[zl	.000	.026	.000	.169	.000	1.0	
[d]	.000	.000	.000	.012	.000	.081	1.0

Anyway, now we're back to map-making, except instead of mapping the relative locations of Dutch cities in geographic space, we're ready to map the perceptual space of English fricatives and "d." Table 4.2 shows the similarities calculated from the Miller and Nicely confusion matrix (table 4.1) using equation (4.1).

The perceptual map based on these similarities is shown in figure 4.4. One of the first things to notice about this map is that the voiced consonants are on one side and the voiceless consonants are on the other. This captures the observation that we made earlier, looking at the raw confusions, that voiceless sounds were rarely called voiced, and vice versa. It is also interesting that the voiced and voiceless fricatives are ordered in the same way on the vertical axis. This might be a front/back dimension, or there might be an interesting correlation with some acoustic aspect of the sounds.

In figure 4.4, I drew ovals around some clusters of sounds. These show two levels of similarity among the sounds as revealed by a hierarchical cluster ana-

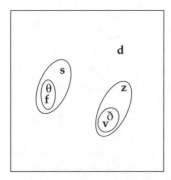

Figure 4.4 The perceptual map of fricatives and [d] in English. The location of the points was determined by multidimensional scaling of the confusion data from Miller and Nicely (1955). The circled groups of sounds are clusters that were found in a hierarchical cluster analysis of the same data.

MDS and acoustic phonetics

In acoustic phonetics one of our fundamental puzzles has been how to decide which aspects of the acoustic speech signal are important and which things don't matter. You look at a spectrogram and see a blob – the question is, do listeners care whether that part of the sound is there? Does that blob matter? Phoneticians have approached the "does it matter?" problem in a number of ways.

For example, we have looked at lots of spectrograms and asked concerning the mysterious blob – "is it always there?" One of the established facts of phonetics is that if an acoustic feature is always, or even usually, present then listeners will expect it in perception. This is even true of the so-called "spit spikes" in the lateral fricatives [ɬ] and [ɮ]. These sounds get a bit juicy, but this somewhat tangential aspect of their production seems to be useful in perception.

Another answer to "does it matter?" has been to identify the origin of the blob in the acoustic theory of speech production. For example, sometimes room reverberation can "add" shadows to a spectrogram. (Actually in the days of reel-to-reel tape recorders we had to be careful of magnetic shadows that crop up when the magnetic sound image transfers across layers of tape on the reel.) If you have a theory of the relationship between speech production and speech acoustics you can answer the question by saying, "it doesn't matter because the talker didn't produce it." We'll be exploring the acoustic theory of speech production in some depth in the remaining chapters of this book.

One of my favorite answers to "does it matter?" is "Cooper's rule." Franklin Cooper, in his 1951 paper with Al Liberman and John Borst, commented on the problem of discovering "the acoustic correlates of perceived speech." They claimed that there are "many questions about the relation between acoustic stimulus and auditory perception which cannot be answered merely by an inspection of spectrograms, no matter how numerous and varied these might be" (an important point for speech technologists to consider). Instead they suggested that "it will often be necessary to make controlled modifications in the spectrogram, and then to evaluate the effects of these modifications on the sound as heard. For these purposes we have constructed an instrument . . ." (one of the first speech synthesizers). This is a pretty beautiful direct answer. Does that blob matter? Well, leave it out when you synthesize the utterance and see if it sounds like something else.

And finally there is the MDS answer. We map the perceptual space and then look for correlations between dimensions of the map and acoustic properties of interest (like the mysterious blob). If an acoustic feature is tightly correlated with a perceptual dimension then we can say that that feature probably does matter. This approach has the advantages of being based on naturally produced speech, and of allowing the simultaneous exploration of many acoustic parameters.

lysis (another neat data analysis method available in most statistics software packages). At the first level of clustering "θ" and "f" cluster with each other and "v" and "ð" cluster together in the perceptual map. At a somewhat more inclusive level the sibilants are included with their non-sibilant neighbors ("s" joins the voiceless cluster and "z" joins the voiced cluster). The next level of clustering, not shown in the figure, puts [d] with the voiced fricatives.

Combining cluster analysis with multi-dimensional scaling gives us a pretty clear view of the perceptual map. Note that these techniques are largely just data visualization techniques, we did not add any information to what was already in the confusion matrix (though we did decide that a two dimensional space adequately describes the pattern of confusions for these sounds).

Concerning the realizations of "this" and "that" we would have to say that these results indicate that the alternations [ð]–[d] and [ð]–[z] are not driven by auditory/perceptual similarity alone – there are evidently other factors at work – otherwise we would find "vis" and "vat" as realizations of "this" and "that."

4.4   The perceptual map of [place]

Now I'd like to talk about how perceptual maps are different from auditory maps. To make this point let's look at some data reported by Braida, Sekiyama and Dix (1998). They presented audio recordings of test syllables that differed by place of articulation (as in [ba], [da], and [ga]) to a group of Japanese listeners. The tokens were presented in noise, and as table 4.3 shows, listeners made a substantial number of mistakes.

Using Shepard's formulas (equations 4.1 and 4.2) for similarity and distance, we have the following estimated similarities and distances for "b," "d," and "g" in the Braida et al. data:

	S_{ij}	d_{ij}
b–d	.57	.56
b–g	.41	.89
d–g	.62	.47

Table 4.3   [Place] confusions for auditory tokens presented in noise, from Braida, Sekiyama and Dix (1998). The table shows response proportions. So, for example, only 56 percent of the [b] tokens were correctly identified as "b."

	"b"	"d"	"g"
[b]	0.56	0.28	0.15
[d]	0.30	0.46	0.24
[g]	0.25	0.31	0.43

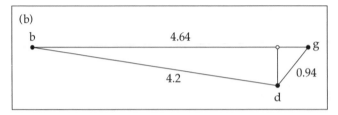

Figure 4.5   Two perceptual maps of place of articulation in Japanese. The data come from Braida, Sekiyama and Dix (1998). (a) A perceptual map derived from the auditory confusion matrix in table 4.3. (b) A perceptual map derived from the visual confusion matrix in table 4.4. In both maps, the position of [d] on the [b]–[g] axis (for a one dimension map) is shown by an open circle.

From these estimates of distance we can draw a perceptual map using triangulation, just like we did when we made part of the geographic map of Holland above. This map of the auditory perceptual space for [b], [d] and [g] is shown in figure 4.5(a). One thing that I've done in this map is to show what it would look like if we "projected" the two dimensional space onto one dimension. This would give us the line from "b" to "g" with "d" located where the open circle is drawn. This one-dimensional projection is not as accurate as the two dimensional map, but below we will find that it is a useful approximation to the auditory perceptual space.

What's interesting about the Braida, Sekiyama and Dix paper is that they also collected visual confusion data for [place]. Here's how to collect visual confusion data. Instead of just making an audio recording of someone saying your test syllables you make a video. Then you can digitize the video and use a digital video editor to chop out little movie clips of the person saying your test words. When you present the video tokens to people for identification responses you turn the volume of the TV or computer all the way down. So they just see a face talking, but can't hear anything.

The Braida et al. visual [place] confusion matrix is shown in table 4.4.

As you can see in the confusion matrix, people are very good at the visual identification of labials, but tend to confuse coronals and dorsals. This pattern of confusions leads to a perceptual map (figure 4.5(b)) in which "b" is quite distant from "d" and "g." It is interesting that "d," the more front of the two non-labials, is a little closer to "b."

As with figure 4.5(a) I have indicated in figure 4.5(b) how "d" projects onto the "b"–"g" line for a one-dimensional version of the visual perceptual space.

Table 4.4   The visual confusion matrix from Braida, Sekiyama and Dix (1998). As in table 4.2, the data are presented as proportions.

	"*b*"	"*d*"	"*g*"
[b]	0.98	0.02	0.004
[d]	0.01	0.85	0.13
[g]	0.01	0.43	0.56

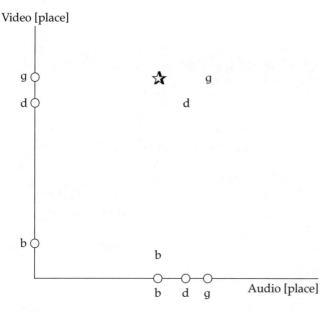

Figure 4.6   The audio-visual perceptual space for consonant place of articulation in Japanese. The horizontal axis shows audio [place] which is the one dimensional projection of the map in figure 4.5(a). The vertical axis shows video [place] which is the one dimensional projection of the map in figure 4.5(b).

Figure 4.6 shows why I wanted to represent these data with one audio dimension and one video dimension (this figure is very much like Braida et al.'s figure 1). In figure 4.6 the audio [place] dimension is on the horizontal axis and the video [place] dimension is on the vertical axis. The phonetic symbols plotted in this two-dimensional map thus show a hypothetical audio-visual perceptual map of [place] in Japanese. It turns out that the actual AV perceptual map (based on perceptual confusions of movies with the sound turned up) is very similar to this predicted AV space.

The star symbol in figure 4.6 shows the location in the perceptual [place] map of a token composed of video [gɑ] and the mismatched audio soundtrack [bɑ].

Why, you may ask, would anyone present such an audio/video mismatch to listeners? I would love to say that McGurk and McDonald (1976) did this to test the validity of the AV [place] map, but actually they were just interested in what would happen. Braida et al. (1998) formulated the hypothesis that the star token tests – namely that listeners have an audio-visual perceptual map for [place] that is a combination of audio and visual maps for [place]. This hypothesis predicts that the mismatch of audio [ba] with video [ga] will result in the perception "da." Interestingly enough, the [ba]$_A$/[ga]$_V$ stimulus does indeed sound like "da." This perceptual illusion is called the "McGurk effect" after Harry McGurk, who first demonstrated it. It is a really surprising effect that only goes away if you close your eyes. Otherwise, even if you know that the audio signal is [ba], you can only hear "da."

McGurking *ad nausea*

The McGurk effect is a really popular phenomenon in speech perception and researchers have poked and prodded it quite a bit to see how it works. In fact it is so popular we can make a verb out of the noun "McGurk effect" – to "McGurk" is to have the McGurk effect. Here are some examples of McGurking:

Babies McGurk – Rosenblum, Schmuckler, and Johnson, 1997
You can McGurk even when the TV is upside down – Campbell, 1994
Japanese listeners McGurk less than English listeners – Sekiyama and Tohkura, 1993
Male faces can McGurk with female voices – Green, Kuhl, Meltzoff and Stevens, 1991
A familiar face with the wrong voice doesn't McGurk – Walker, Bruce and O'Malley, 1995

Let's come back to the main point of this section. Perceptual representations are different from auditory representations. I have tried to show that these two are different from each other by showing a perceptual map that has an auditory dimension on one axis and a visual dimension on the other. Then I suggested that the McGurk effect shows that this perceptual space is the one used by listeners. You "hear" [ba] differently when you see the face saying [ga]. This means that the perceptual representation of speech has both auditory and visual aspects.

4.5   The limits of perceptual universality:
A cross-linguistic map of Chinese tones

This section is about another way that perception is different from audition. It is reasonable to believe that the functioning of the auditory system is not affected by native language. The bones of the middle ear may vary from person to person (particularly if you've had serious ear infections) and the physiology of the inner ear may vary, but there is no reason to believe that language experience causes auditory system changes. The same is not true of speech perception. Instead, we need to be able to distinguish aspects of perception that may be universal, having a firm basis in pure audition or vision, from aspects of perception that show the effects of linguistic tuning.

A substantial body of research leads to the conclusion that people who speak different languages have different perceptual maps. To illustrate the language specificity of speech perception (the limits of perceptual universality) we will consider some data from a recent study of Mandarin Chinese tones (Huang, 2001).

Mandarin Chinese has four distinctive tones – these are particular pitch patterns that appear on stressed syllables. In IPA notation they are: the high tone, [55]; the falling tone, [51]; the rising tone, [35]; and the dipping tone, [214] which is usually realized as [21] (remember this little fact). One of the phonological rules of Mandarin is a tone rule that in a sequence of two dipping tones the first one changes into a rising tone.

214 214 → 35 214

Huang (2001) agreed with researchers who have suggested that this change makes the sequence of tones easier to say, but she raised the question of why the rising tone in particular is chosen to replace the first dipping tone, rather than choosing one of the other two tones [55] or [51]. She hypothesized that the change 214 → 35 is "a case of perceptually tolerated articulatory simplification" because tone 35 is perceptually similar to tone 214.

This Mandarin tone rule is an old one – perhaps first appearing in the language 700 years ago. We know it is old because many related "dialects" of Mandarin have the rule, even though they have been separated from each other for a long time. Therefore, it is a matter of some speculation to say that the tone shapes were 35 and 214 at the time that the rule came into the language. Chen (1976) suggested that these tones both had a rising contour, and on this dimension differed from the other tones of Mandarin. My assumption, based on Chen (1976), is that the tones were shaped at least approximately like 35 and 214 when the tone rule first appeared, and that Huang's study is therefore a direct test of the role of perception in the historical development of this pattern in Mandarin.

At any rate, Huang conducted a study to map the perceptual space of tones in Mandarin and that's our main focus here. Her study goes beyond the methods that we've seen so far in this chapter. First, she determined the perceptual map for both native speakers of Mandarin Chinese and for American English speakers. It was important to test listeners who don't speak Chinese because of the phonological rule that converts 214 into 35 in Chinese. This rule relating the tones might influence their position in a perceptual map, so that the effect is taken to be the cause. In other words, they might be confusable because of the rule, instead of the rule being caused or permitted by perceptual confusability. To conduct the test in American English Huang needed to refrain from use of the identification task. This is because her English listeners didn't know the names of the Chinese tones and she didn't want to try to teach them Chinese as a part of the experiment. Therefore, and this is her second methodological extension, she used a discrimination task and measured reaction time.

A trial in her experiment went like this. The listener heard two syllables, call them syllable A and syllable X. A and X always matched on their consonant and vowel, they only differed by which of the tones they had. If A and X where simply repetitions of the same syllable – same tone – then the listener was supposed to press a button labeled "same." But if A and X had different tones then the listener was supposed to press the "different" button. The buttons were connected to a computer that was clocking the amount of time it took to respond "same" or "different." Huang used the reaction time for correct "different" responses as a measure of the perceptual similarity of the two tones.

We think it is OK to use reaction time as a measure of similarity because it makes sense to believe that if two things are similar to each other it will take longer to notice that they are actually different. And we know of some prior research that bears this assumption out (e.g. Shepard, Kilpatrick and Cunningham, 1975).

Huang's data are shown in table 4.5. In this table we see for example that for Mandarin listeners it took 563 milliseconds to answer "different" when the high level tone [55] and the rising tone [35] were presented. We see right away that the longest average reaction times for both Mandarin and English listeners occured when [35] and [214] were paired with each other (these times are underlined in the table). Following Shepard et al. (1975) Huang then calculated distance from the reaction times by simply taking the inverse of the time. Thus, the distance between [55] and [35] for Mandarin listeners was assumed to be 1.776 (= 1/0.563).

This gives us a matrix of distances from our matrix of reaction times, so we can use multidimensional scaling to map the perceptual space just as we did in the previous sections of this chapter. The perceptual tone spaces of Mandarin and English listeners are shown in figure 4.7. Notice in figure 4.7 that the American English tone space fits inside the Mandarin Chinese tone space. This aspect of the data is also apparent in the reaction times in table 4.5 (recalling that perceptual map-making is mainly a way of visualizing patterns in data). On average the English listeners took longer (609 ms) than Chinese listeners (584 ms) to choose

Table 4.5 Average reaction times (in milliseconds) for correct "different" responses in Huang's (2001) study of tone perception.

(a) Mandarin listeners					(b) American English listeners			
	[55]	[35]	[214]	[51]		[55]	[35]	[214]	[51]
[55]					[55]				
[35]	563				[35]	615			
[214]	579	683			[214]	536	706		
[51]	588	548	545		[51]	600	592	608	

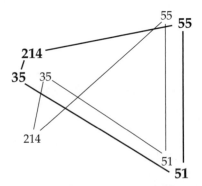

Figure 4.7 Maps of the perceptual tone spaces for Mandarin Chinese listeners (heavy lines, large font) and American English listeners (light lines, small font). These maps were produced by linear multi-dimensional scaling of the data in table 4.5. The MDS dimensions were scaled by the regression coefficent relating actual and predicted distance so that distance in the MDS solution is proportional to distance in the raw data. The lines drawn in this figure show some selected perceptual distances – e.g. the distance between tone [55] and tone [214] is shown as a line for both the Mandarin and American English listeners, while the [55]–[35] distance is not directly drawn in for either group.

"different" when the tones didn't match. This indicates that the tones were less distinct for the English listeners, on average – hence a smaller perceptual space.

Note also that the dipping tone [214] is closer to the rising [35] tone than any other tone for both the Chinese listeners and the English listeners. Huang was right that the rising tone is more confusable with the dipping tone and thus more likely to replace it in a phonological rule. Interestingly, the distance between tone [214] and tone [35] is shorter for Chinese listeners, despite their overall larger tone space. This suggests that the phonological relationship between the tones (that [214] → [35] sometimes) decreased their separation in the Chinese perceptual space.

Finally, what about that odd crossing pattern in the American English tone space? The horizontal dimension is the same for both groups of listeners – tones that start with high pitch are on the right side of the map and tones that start relatively low are on the left side. But the vertical dimension codes different things for the two groups. Now is when it is important to remember that the dipping tone [214] is most often simplified to [21]. For Chinese listeners the vertical dimension distinguishes the basically level tones [55] and [21] from the contour tones [35] and [51]. Perhaps it is no coincidence that Chinese scholars call Mandarin Chinese a "contour tone language." For English listeners, though, the vertical dimension codes a simpler phonetic property – the pitch at the end of the syllable – distinguishing the tones that end low [21] and [51] from the tones that end high [55] and [35]. I think that this is a mighty cool result!

Remember the main point of this section, which was also one of the main points of this chapter, language experience alters your perception of language. Experience changes your perceptual map for speech, tuning it to better perceive the contrasts and structure of your language.

Exercises

Sufficient jargon

test syllable versus test token, confusion matrix, identification task, signal to noise ratio, reaction time, multi-dimensional scaling, perceptual distance, projection, triangulation, McGurk effect.

Short answer questions

1 Randomize the order of this list of words. Describe your method.
     "one," "two," "three," "four," "five," "six," "seven," "eight"
2 Use a ruler and a compass to draw the perceptual space that is encoded in the following matrix of distances. Note, this is a matrix of the perceived differences in talker's voices. We played pairs of words to listeners and asked them "does it sound like the same person twice or two different people?" Then we measured similarity as the number of times that different talkers were called the "same." The distance values in this table were then calculated by equation 4.2. So listeners responded "same" 15 percent of the time when they heard talker AJ paired with talker CN [$1.9 = -\ln(0.15)$]. Can you tell which two of the talkers are twins?

	AJ	CN	NJ	RJ
AJ		1.9	0.3	1.9
CN	1.9		2.3	2.5
NJ	0.3	2.3		1.9
RJ	1.9	2.5	1.9	

3 Compute the perceptual distance between "ð" and "d" in table 4.1. Is "ð" closer to "d" or "z"?
4 Now that we think of perceptual maps as having audio and video dimensions we can reconsider the failure of our perceptual explanation for the variants of "this" and "that". In particular, could the visual component somehow explain why we see no "vis" or "vat" as variants of "this" and "that"? What audio-visual perceptual space (or spaces) could possibly give rise to reduced [v]/ [ð] confusions yet still permit Keif for "Keith"?
5 You may have noticed that in this chapter I used some different notations to refer to speech sounds. Here are the interpretations that were implicitly in the text:

     [θ] – phonetic articulatory or acoustic physical aspects of the sound
     [θ]$_A$ – phonetic aspects conveyed acoustically
     [θ]$_V$ – phonetic aspects conveyed visually
     "θ" – the perceptual representation of the sound

     Some researchers argue that perceptual representations like "θ" are of speech gestures – i.e. that listeners interpret speech in terms of vocal tract activities rather than simply in terms of sensory patterns. What in this chapter is compatible or incompatible with this "gesturalist" view of speech perception?
6 One theory of speech perception claims that the ability to perceive speech is genetically prespecified. In some quarters, this has been taken to mean that humans have innate "feature detectors" used in perceiving speech. How do Huang's (2001) data on tone perception challenge this view?

CHAPTER 5

The Acoustic Theory of Speech Production: Deriving Schwa

Vocal fold vibration is the usual source of sound in vowels, and the vocal tract is an acoustic filter that modifies the sound made by the vocal folds. This account of speech acoustics is known as the source-filter theory of speech production (Fant, 1960; Flanagan, 1965). This chapter describes the sound produced by vocal fold vibration, digresses briefly to introduce Stevens's (1972, 1989) quantal theory, and then discusses the filtering action of the vocal tract in the production of schwa [ə]. The acoustic theory of speech production, as the name implies, is a theory not just of schwa, and the concepts introduced in this chapter will come up repeatedly in the following chapters.

5.1   Voicing

When the vocal folds vibrate, they produce a complex periodic wave. Figure 5.1 shows a voicing waveform produced by a (very natural-sounding) speech synthesizer. Note that the voicing waveform has a nonsinusoidal repeating pattern. The number of times that this complex periodic waveform repeats per second determines its fundamental frequency (F_0), and is related to the listener's perception of the pitch of the voice. In this case each cycle is 6.66 ms long, so the fundamental frequency is 150 Hz (1 second/0.0066 seconds).

A Fourier analysis of the voicing waveform gives us a power spectrum that shows the component frequencies and their amplitudes (figure 5.2). The fundamental frequency is the first (lowest-frequency) peak in the power spectrum, and each of the other peaks in the spectrum is at a multiple of the fundamental frequency. So, for example, the second peak in the spectrum occurs at 300 Hz, the third at 450 Hz, and the tenth at 1,500 Hz. The components of the voicing spectrum

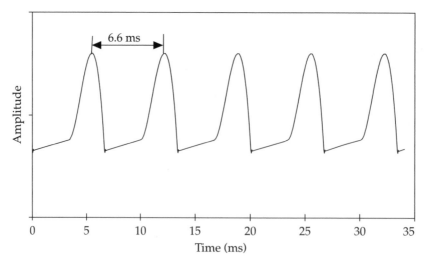

Figure 5.1   Five cycles from the voice source of a speech synthesizer (Klatt and Klatt, 1990). This waveform serves as the input to an acoustic simulation of the vocal tract to produce synthetic vowel sounds. The fundamental frequency is 150 Hz; each cycle takes 6.6 ms.

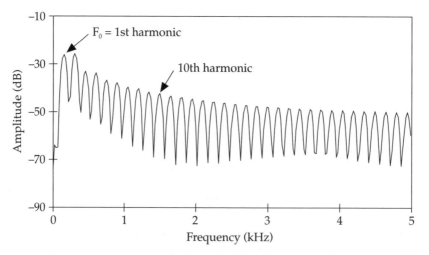

Figure 5.2   A power spectrum of the vocal cord vibration shown in figure 5.1. The first harmonic (which has the same frequency as the fundamental frequency of voicing) occurs at 150 Hz; therefore the tenth harmonic occurs at 1,500 Hz.

are called **harmonics**. Note that the amplitude of each harmonic above the second is a little less than the one just below it in frequency. (The relative amplitudes of the first and second harmonics are related to phonation type – see figure 8.3.)

Here is an illustration of what harmonics are. (John Ohala objects to this illustration because vocal fold vibration produces sound the way a siren does, by modulating an airstream. However, I've been unable to come up with a better way to illustrate how harmonics are modes of vibration, even if in the case of a vibrating string the modes of vibration are really the resonant frequencies of the string. So let the reader beware; the illustration is not entirely apt.) When you pluck a guitar

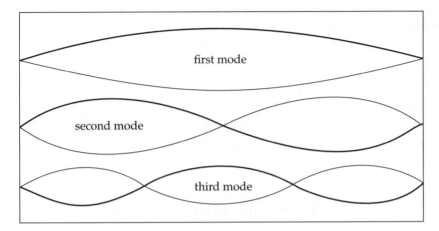

Figure 5.3   Three modes of vibration of a plucked string. The top pair of lines shows the patterns of maximal displacement of the first mode; the next pair shows the maximal displacement patterns of the second mode; and the bottom pair shows the maximal displacement patterns of the third mode.

string, it vibrates, and produces a sound that is similar in some ways to voicing. The guitar string vibration is a complex periodic sound with a fundamental frequency and higher-frequency harmonic components that are multiples of the fundamental frequency. The note's harmonics (including the fundamental frequency) result from the large number of ways in which a guitar string can vibrate. Figure 5.3 illustrates three of these modes of vibration. The top trace in the figure shows the lowest-frequency mode of vibration. The whole string oscillates up and down at a frequency which is determined by the length of the string. This mode determines the fundamental frequency of the guitar string, and hence the pitch of the note.

The second trace in the figure shows the second mode of vibration. As in the first mode (and as is true for any mode of vibration of a guitar string), the ends of the string do not move; but in this mode the string's length is divided in two. While half of the string is moving one way, the other half moves the opposite way, and there is a point in the middle of the string, called a "node," that doesn't move at all. Because the frequency of vibration of a string is determined by its length, and in the second mode of vibration the string is divided in half, the frequency of the second mode is twice that of the first mode – that is, twice the fundamental frequency.

The bottom trace in figure 5.3 shows the third mode of vibration of a guitar string. In this mode the string is divided into thirds. As before, the ends of the string do not move (this is called a "boundary condition" for the modes of vibration, and we will see this idea again when we talk about the filtering action of the vocal tract). Since the length of each vibrating section of the string is one-third the total length of the string, the third mode of vibration gives rise to a component in the complex wave (the third harmonic) that is three times the fundamental frequency.

There is a way to hear the second harmonic of a guitar string. You can pluck the string and then lightly touch the middle of the string. When you do this, the sound changes in two ways: its amplitude decreases, and its pitch doubles. The first and third harmonics are damped when you touch the middle of the string (at points of maximum displacement in these modes of vibration), while the second harmonic, which comes from the second mode of vibration., is not. All odd-numbered harmonics are damped when you touch the middle of the string, so that only the even-numbered harmonics remain.

The modes of vibration of a guitar string provide a simple illustration of the relationship between the fundamental frequency and the harmonics of a complex periodic wave. Vocal fold vibration is more complicated, but the relationships among the components of the voicing waveform are much the same. Vocal fold vibration gives rise to a complex periodic sound having harmonics that are integral multiples of the fundamental frequency.

5.2   Voicing quanta

The action of the vocal folds provides one of the clearest examples of the **quantal theory** of speech, so we will take a brief detour into quantal theory at this point. Stevens (1972) proposed quantal theory to account for the fact that languages do not use the full range of possible speech articulations. Numerous possible articulations are rarely, if ever, used in any language to distinguish words. He suggested that this is because the mapping between articulation and acoustics is nonlinear. Articulation of the vocal folds is a good example of this nonlinearity. During speech the opening between the vocal folds (the glottis) varies from wide open (as when you take a deep breath) to pressed tightly shut (as in a glottal stop). This continuous range of glottal widths is represented on the horizontal axis of figure 5.4.

The acoustic consequences (assuming a constant amount of air pressure below the vocal cords) of gradually changing the glottal width from open to closed are

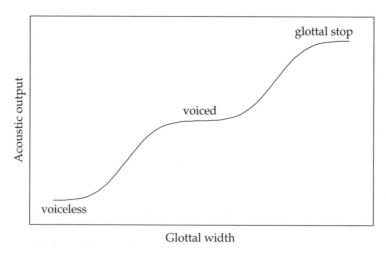

Figure 5.4   Quantal regions in the relationship between glottal width and the acoustic output of the glottis are represented as plateaus.

Quantal theory and radio knobs

Quantal theory is based on the idea that the nonlinear mapping between articulation and acoustics defines the distinctive features used in language. This raises the question, "What does nonlinear mean?"

Linear control is like the volume knob on a radio. Turn the knob, and the sound gets louder (or softer). The further you turn the knob, the greater the change in volume. Nonlinear control is like the tuning knob of the radio. As you turn this knob, the radio recieves different stations. So a small turn of the knob may result in a large change in the sound produced by the radio, and a large turn may cause very little change (all static).

shown on the vertical axis in the figure. The articulatory dimension in this example, glottal width, is something of an abstraction, in that it encompasses both the area of the glottis and tension in the muscles that close the glottis and the vocal folds themselves. At first, when the vocal folds are open, the fricative [h] is produced; but then, at some critical width, a quantal change occurs in the acoustic output, and the vocal folds start to vibrate. The vibration may be somewhat breathy (as in the [ɦ] of *ahead*), but the type of sound produced is completely different from before. There is another abrupt change in acoustic output when the glottis closes, producing a glottal stop. So glottal width is like the tuning control on a radio, rather than the volume control; a small change can produce a large effect.

Stevens argues that nonlinear relationships between articulation and acoustics such as this are exploited by languages. The horizontal segments in the trace in figure 5.4 labeled "voiceless," "voiced," and "glottal stop" are *regions of stability* in the articulation-to-acoustics mapping. For example, speakers can choose any one of several possible glottal widths and still produce voicing. A certain amount of articulatory slop can be tolerated, because a whole range of different glottal widths produce practically the same output. In this way, the natural nonlinearity in the mapping from articulation to acoustic output leads to natural classes of speech sounds. A full inventory of nonlinearities in the articulation-to-acoustics mapping would express, in Stevens's view, the inventory of distinctive phonetic features that can be used to distinguish meaning in language. In the case of vocal cord activity, the regions of stability (the "quantal" regions) are easy to identify. We will see some other cases in which the argument is a little more subtle than this.

5.3   Vocal tract filtering

The vocal tract can function as a filter to change the voicing waveform shown in figure 5.1 into a complex periodic waveform like the one shown in figure 5.5. I made this figure by playing the synthetic voicing component shown in figure 5.1

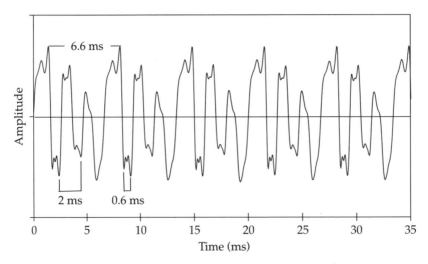

Figure 5.5 Acoustic waveform of a synthetic schwa. The period durations of three prominent components are identified.

through a set of band-pass filters. The resulting synthetic vowel sounds like schwa [ə], the vowel in the first syllable of *ahead* in American English. The fundamental frequency still has a period of 6.6 ms, so the waveform pattern repeats itself 150 times per second, but in this waveform it is possible to identify some other prominent oscillatory components. For instance, within each period there is a component that repeats once every 2 ms, and thus has a frequency of 500 Hz. Note also that there is an even faster-moving oscillation that is easiest to see as a double-peaked pattern in the waveform overlaid on some of the 2 ms peaks. This oscillation repeats once every 0.666 ms (the distance between the double peaks), and thus has a frequency of 1,500 Hz.

The spectrum of the voicing source (shown in figure 5.2) and the spectrum of schwa shown in figure 5.6 have the same fundamental frequencies (as indicated by the harmonics at 150 Hz, 300 Hz, 450 Hz, etc.). So both sounds are composed of the same harmonics, but the relative amplitudes of the harmonics are different. In the spectrum of the voice source, the harmonics decrease steadily in amplitude as their frequency increases; while in the spectrum of schwa the harmonics around 500 Hz, 1,500 Hz, 2,500 Hz, and 3,500 Hz have higher amplitudes than harmonics at other frequencies. As we saw in the waveform in figure 5.5, these seemingly minor changes in the relative amplitudes of the harmonics have a major impact on the shape of the waveform.

The broad spectral peaks, for which we have evidence in both the waveform and the spectrum, were in this case (i.e. this synthetic schwa) produced by playing the voice source waveform through a set of band-pass filters with center frequencies at 500 Hz, 1,500 Hz, 2,500 Hz, and 3,500 Hz. The fact that such a method of speech synthesis produces an intelligible vowel sound suggests that the vocal tract also functions like a set of band-pass filters.

Figure 5.6   The power spectrum of the vowel sound shown in figure 5.5. Note that the harmonics have the same frequencies that they had in the voicing spectrum (figure 5.2) – for example, the tenth harmonic has a frequency of 1,500 Hz. However, the relative amplitudes of the harmonics are not the same; in the spectrum of schwa there are broad spectral peaks near 500 Hz, 1,500 Hz, 2,500 Hz, and 3,500 Hz.

5.4   Pendulums, standing waves, and vowel formants

The acoustic properties of schwa can be simulated by a bank of band-pass filters, because the vocal tract has resonant frequencies. Harmonics in the voice source that have nearly the same frequency as the vocal tract resonances are enhanced (as if they were in the pass-band of a filter), and components of the source that do not have frequencies near a resonance are damped.

The resonant frequency of a pendulum

The resonant frequencies in schwa are caused by standing waves in the vocal tract. The oscillation of a pendulum illustrates some properties of resonance which are useful to consider in this context. Try this experiment. Fix a weight to a string, and see how it swings (you can use a shoelace and a spoon). If you hold the end of the string in one hand and with the other pull the weight to one side and release it, it will oscillate to and fro for a while. Notice that the amount of time it takes to swing through one to-and-fro cycle is independent of the magnitude of the swing. You can also make the weight swing by moving your wrist. If you move your wrist from side to side with the right timing, the pendulum will eventually swing in large arcs. Note that the size of the arcs is much larger than the movement of your wrist, but only if the timing is right;

if you move your wrist too quickly or too slowly, the weight will tend to stay in place rather than swing.

Why does it matter how quickly or how slowly you swing the pendulum? Note that the amount of time it takes to complete one swing is invariant; each cycle takes the same amount of time to complete, regardless of whether you have just started to get it to swing by making small wrist movements, or whether you are vigorously swinging it with large movements of your arm, or if you have simply nudged the weight with one hand while holding the end of the string stationary. This indicates that the pendulum has a particular resonant frequency. Notice that if you shorten the string, the duration of the period decreases. You can also verify the importance of the length of the string by comparing the resonant frequencies of pendulums of different weights (for instance, compare a spoon to a hammer). So the pendulum has a natural resonant frequency. If you introduce energy (wrist movements) into the system at about the resonant frequency, then the system will enhance that energy by adding each successive bit of energy introduced into the system (your wrist movements, if properly timed, will be added to each other), but if you introduce energy at some other frequency, the system will damp the energy, because it is canceled by the previous energy pulses.

So each movement of your wrist introduces a small amount of energy into the pendulum. The timing of the movements is the frequency at which energy is introduced to the system, and the swinging of the pendulum (or lack of it) is the result of coupling between the energy source and the resonant system.

Here's an acoustic example of resonance. Suppose you took a tube and placed a loudspeaker at one end and a cap over the other, and played a sine wave through the loudspeaker. Figure 5.7 illustrates the response of the acoustic tube as the sine wave begins to come out of the loudspeaker. Air pressure in this figure is indicated by shading, where atmospheric pressure is gray, compression is black, and rarefaction is white. A pressure peak moves from just outside the speaker at time 1 to the end of the tube at time 3. At time 4 the pressure peak has reflected from the capped end of the tube, while the pressure valley which appeared at time 3 near the loudspeaker has progressed to the middle of the tube. The two cancel, and thus the pressure at all points in the tube is equal to atmospheric pressure. At time 5 the positive pressure peak returns to the loudspeaker, while the pressure valley reaches the cap at the opposite end of the tube. Now if the sine wave coming out of the loudspeaker is of the right frequency, a new pressure peak will be added to the reflection of the first. (Actually, the frequency of the sine wave is crucial to the timing of the pressure valley at time 3 as well.) So, at time 5 we have a pressure peak at the loudspeaker end of the tube that is a combination of the reflected peak and the new peak being emitted by the speaker – like pushing a child on a swing. With each cycle of the sine wave, the pressure peak has a higher amplitude, and the pressure valley is lower. I haven't

Figure 5.7 The first cycle of a sine wave played into an acoustic tube closed at both ends (where one end is closed by a loudspeaker). The bands labeled 1–5 show air pressure in the tube at five different times. Pressure is indicated by degree of darkness, where black is compression, white is rarefaction, and gray is zero (atmospheric) pressure.

actually constructed a device like this, but one wonders if it would explode after a few cycles.

At subsequent times there will be an oscillation between the states represented at times 3 and 5, with intervals like the state at time 4 in between. This can be seen in figure 5.8a, which shows the first resonance of an acoustic tube, such as we have been discussing, which is closed at both ends. The times labeled 1–5 correspond to the shaded bars in figure 5.7. The oscillating pattern in the tube "stands still" in the tube in the sense that the point in the middle always has zero pressure, while pressure oscillates between peaks and valleys at either end of the tube.

In figure 5.8 I use a notation to represent sine waves whereby + stands for the pressure peaks in the wave, 0 for the points where the wave crosses zero ampli-tude, – for the pressure valleys in the wave, and ± for the zero pressure that results when a peak and a valley cancel each other.

If you look down the column of pressure values at the loudspeaker end of the tube in figure 5.8a you will see the oscillation between peaks and valleys in the sine wave being emitted by the loudspeaker. In addition, starting at time 4, there is a regularly repeating pressure pattern in the tube. At odd-numbered times there is a pressure peak at one end of the tube and a pressure valley at the other,

(a) First resonance

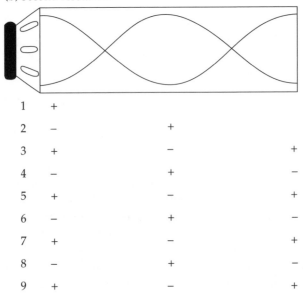

1	+		
2	0	+	
3	−	0	+
4	0	±	0
5	+	0	−
6	0	±	0
7	−	0	+
8	0	±	0
9	+	0	−

(b) Second resonance

1	+		
2	−	+	
3	+	−	+
4	−	+	−
5	+	−	+
6	−	+	−
7	+	−	+
8	−	+	−
9	+	−	+

Figure 5.8 Standing waves of the two lowest resonant frequencies of a tube closed at both ends with a loudspeaker at one end. Time is shown vertically from earlier (1) to later (9). Pressure peaks are represented by plus (+), pressure valleys by minus (−), and zero, atmospheric pressure, by zero (0) or in the case of canceling peaks and valleys by plus-minus (±). (a) shows the first resonance corresponding to the wave shown in figure 5.7, (b) the next higher resonant frequency of the tube, and (c) the pattern produced by a nonresonant frequency.

(c) A nonresonant frequency

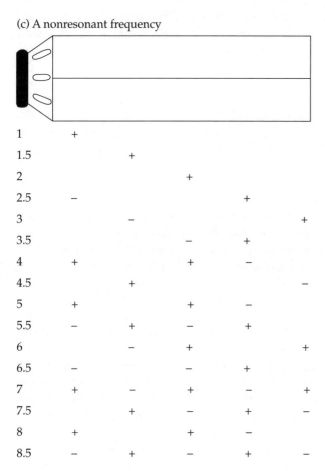

Time					
1	+				
1.5		+			
2			+		
2.5	−			+	
3		−			+
3.5			−	+	
4	+		+	−	
4.5		+			−
5	+		+	−	
5.5	−	+	−	+	
6		−	+		+
6.5	−		−	+	
7	+	−	+	−	+
7.5		+	−	+	−
8	+		+	−	
8.5	−	+	−	+	−

Figure 5.8 *continued*

while at even-numbered times the peak and valley cancel each other at the mid-point of the tube. So at the midpoint of the tube, pressure remains zero, equal to atmospheric pressure, while at the ends of the tube pressure oscillates between positive and negative peaks. This pattern is known as a **standing wave**. The point in the middle of the tube where pressure remains zero is called a **node** in the standing wave, while the points at the ends of the tube where pressure reaches both positive and negative maxima are called **antinodes.**

Notice that there is another way of representing standing waves, also shown in figure 5.8. In this representation standing waves are drawn as two intersecting sinusoidal wave segments in the tube. The waves drawn in the tube in figure 5.8a, for example, correspond to the distribution of pressure values at times 3 and 5. In this representation, nodes are indicated by the intersection of the sine waves, and antinodes by their peaks.

Unlike a pendulum, which is called a "simple harmonic system" because it has only one resonant frequency, acoustic tubes have many resonant frequencies. In figure 5.8, (a) and (b) illustrate the two lowest resonant frequencies in a tube closed at both ends, with (b) showing the response of the tube to a sine wave that has a frequency twice that shown in (a). So, looking down the first column of pluses and minuses, you can see that while in the first resonance (a) the valley in the sine wave occurs at time 3, in the second resonance (b) the sine wave has already completed a cycle by that time. Note that the pressure peak emitted by the loudspeaker travels at the same speed in both resonances; at time 3 the peak reaches the capped end of the tube, and by time 5 it returns to the loudspeaker. Also note that the time it takes for the sound wave to travel to the capped end of the tube, then back, determines the frequencies that will resonate in the tube. Both the first resonance and the second resonance require that at time 5 the sine wave produced by the loudspeaker have a pressure peak. If the tube were longer, and thus the amount of time it took for the wave to travel to the capped end and back were longer, the tube would resonate only to sine waves produced by the loudspeaker that have longer periods (lower frequencies), so that a pressure peak emitted by the loudspeaker would occur, for example, at time 6 rather than time 5.

Let's see what happens when the frequency of the sine wave emitted by the loudspeaker does not match a resonant frequency of the tube. An example is shown in (c) of figure 5.8. What we see here is the result of driving the loudspeaker with a sine wave with a frequency between those shown in (a) and (b); the cycle is four time units (note that, unlike the other cases, time is shown at a resolution of half the time units used previously). In (c) there are a couple of points at which the reflected peak combines with the peak newly emitted by the loudspeaker, and at these same points in the tube the reflected pressure valley combines with the emitted valley. However, they are always moving in opposite directions – that is, they never get added together to form a standing wave of greater amplitude than the one emitted by the loudspeaker. This example shows that, in order for the pressure peaks to add together and form a standing wave, the sine wave emitted by the loudspeaker has to have a peak at time 5 (the point when the reflected wave will have made its way back to the loudspeaker).

Wavelength

If you want to know whether a sine wave will resonate in a tube, you need to know the distance that it travels in a cycle. This distance is called its **wavelength**. You can visualize wavelength by imagining that the wave illustrated in figure 5.7 did not reflect off the end of the tube, but just kept on going down a long tube. To calculate the wavelength, we start with the duration of the sine wave's period. Recall that the interval in time between successive peaks in the waveform (for instance, the interval between times 1 and 5 in figure 5.7) is the period (T). The wavelength (λ) depends on the speed of sound in the tube. (You may recognize the problem in a slightly different form: how far can you travel if your speed is 30 miles per hour and your time spent traveling at that speed is one hour?) In warm, moist air the speed of sound (c) is about 35,000 centimeters per second (cm/s). So the wavelength is the duration of one period multiplied by the speed of sound ($\lambda = cT$), or, equivalently, because frequency is the inverse of the period ($1/T = f$), wavelength is equal to the speed of sound divided by the frequency of the sine wave ($\lambda = c/f$). For example, a 1,000 Hz sine wave has a period duration of 1 millisecond, or 0.001 seconds. So its wavelength is $35,000 \times 0.001 = 35,000/1,000 = 35$ cm. That is, successive peaks in a 1,000 Hz sine wave are 35 cm apart, so if you took two microphones and placed them 35 cm apart and played a 1,000 Hz sine wave near them, the microphones would, for any instant of time, pick up the same point in the phase of the wave; whereas if the microphones were 17.5 cm apart, one would record a peak at the time that the other records a valley. Both microphones would pick up a sine wave, but the relative phase would depend on the distance between them because of the wavelength.

So, in the case we have been considering (a tube closed at both ends), sine waves that will produce standing waves in the tube are those that "fit" in the tube. That is, the sine waves that fit will travel to and fro in the tube in such a way that they have either a peak or a valley at the loudspeaker end of the tube at the same time that a matching pressure value is being emitted by the speaker. If you know the length of the tube and the speed of sound in air, you can calculate the frequencies that will produce standing waves (i.e. the resonant frequencies of the tube). The wavelength of the first resonance (λ) is twice the length of the tube (2L), half of the length being taken up by the movement from the loudspeaker to the cap, the other half by the return trip. The resonant frequency is therefore the speed of sound divided by the wavelength ($f = c/2L$). For example, if the tube is 8 cm long, then the wavelength of the first resonance is 16 cm, and thus the frequency is $35,000/16 = 2,187.5$ Hz. All higher resonances of the tube are simply multiples of the first resonant frequency. For instance, the wavelength of the second resonance (see figure 5.8b) is half the wavelength of the first resonance, so the second resonant frequency of an 8 cm long tube is $f_2 = c/L$, and in general the resonant frequencies of a tube that is closed at both ends can be calculated by equation (5.1) below, where n is the resonance number, c is the speed of sound, and L is the length of the tube. So a tube 8 cm long closed at both ends has resonant frequencies of 2,187.5 Hz, 4,375 Hz, 6,562.5 Hz, and so on.

$$f_n = nc/2L \qquad\qquad\qquad (5.1)$$

Now suppose that the loudspeaker was emitting a complex wave, rather than a sine wave. We know from chapter 2 that a complex wave is a combination of a number of component sine waves. So the only difference between the examples that we have been considering in figure 5.8 and a complex wave is that numerous sine waves are injected into the tube simultaneously. So, rather than considering

(a) Second resonance

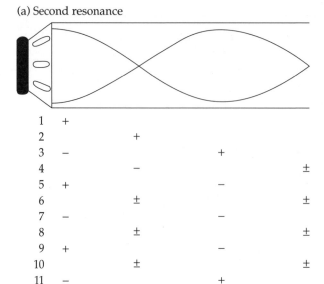

1	+		
2		+	
3	−		+
4		−	±
5	+		−
6		±		±
7	−		−
8		±		±
9	+		−
10		±		±
11	−		+
12		±		±
13	+		−

(b) First resonance

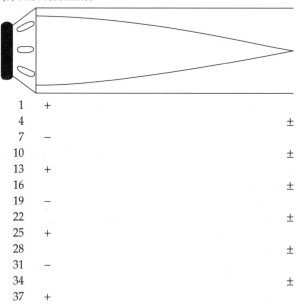

1	+	
4		±
7	−	
10		±
13	+	
16		±
19	−	
22		±
25	+	
28		±
31	−	
34		±
37	+	

Figure 5.9 Standing waves of the two lowest resonant frequencies of a tube closed by a loudspeaker at one end and open at the other. Time is shown vertically from earlier to later. Pressure peaks are represented by plus (+), pressure valleys by minus (−), and zero, atmospheric pressure, in the case of canceling peaks and valleys by plus-minus (±). (a) shows the second resonance, (b) the first resonance, of the tube.

the resonance properties of the tube by exploring the tube response to different sine waves in sequence, we can have a combination of all the waves illustrated in figure 5.8 and more. I can't think of a way to illustrate this in terms of waves bouncing around in the tube, because the situation is too complex. However, We can make some predictions. First, we predict that if the complex sound source contains frequencies near the resonant frequencies of the tube (such as the two illustrated in figures 5.8a and b), the amplitudes of these components of the source will be enhanced. Second, we predict that if the complex sound source contains frequencies not near the resonant frequencies of the tube, then the amplitudes of these components will be damped. Hence, although this section illustrated standing waves by talking about how sine waves behave in a tube, the discussion is relevant to acoustic speech analysis because the complex voicing waveform can be analyzed as a set of sine waves.

There is one other way in which the illustration of standing waves given above differs from normal speech production. I have assumed for the sake of illustration a tube that is closed at both ends. Obviously, in schwa, as well as in most other speech sounds, we are interested in the acoustics of tubes that are open at one end. The only acoustic difference between a tube that is closed at both ends and a tube that is closed at only one end concerns how sound waves reflect from the open end of the tube. It may be hard to realize intuitively that sound is reflected from the open end of the tube, but it is. This happens because the sound wave strikes a big immobile mass of air that is sitting just outside the lip of the tube. You may have experienced this sort of sound reflection without realizing it when, for example, someone leans across the seat of a car to talk to you through the open window. The window is like the open end of a tube, and much of the acoustic energy in the speech signal is reflected back into the car rather than traveling on to the outside. Although the person may be speaking clearly, you can hardly hear them.

So, sound waves reflect back into the tube from the open end. However, the type of reflection at the open end is different from that at the closed end. The difference is that the sign of the sound wave changes, so that a peak is reflected from the open end of the tube as a valley. An example of this type of polarity change is the crack made by a bull whip (a long strip of braided leather on a short handle). To crack the whip, you send a wave down its length. When the wave reaches the end of the whip, which is analogous to the open end of a tube because it isn't attached to anything, it undergoes a sudden polarity change, which produces a loud crack! The polarity change in the reflection of sound waves at the open end of a tube does not produce a loud noise, but it does alter the resonant frequencies of the tube substantially.

Figure 5.9 illustrates, in the style of figure 5.8, the two lowest resonant frequencies of a tube that is open at one end. Look first at the second resonant frequency (a). Tracing the pressure peak emitted by the loudspeaker at time 1, we see that it reaches the end of the tube at time 4 (for the sake of illustration I used a different time scale in this figure as compared with figure 5.8), and undergoes a polarity shift from + to −. One consequence of this is that, in this standing wave, the pressure at the tube's opening is always zero, because the peak becomes a valley at this point, and the two cancel each other. Because of the polarity shift at the open end of the tube the pressure peak emitted by the loudspeaker at time 1 returns to the loudspeaker as a pressure valley at time 7, travels back to the open end, undergoes a polarity shift again, and travels back to the loudspeaker by time 13. So the lowest resonant frequency of the tube will have a period of 12. This is illustrated in figure 5.9b, which has a compressed time scale. The sine wave emitted by the loudspeaker must have the frequency shown in the first column of (b) in order to match the pressure peak or valley reflected from the open end of the tube; the reflected wave must travel the length of the tube four times before it returns to the loudspeaker as a pressure peak. This means that the wavelength of the first resonant frequency is four times the length of the tube (4L).

Figure 5.9a shows the second resonant frequency and illustrates that in this type of tube the relationship between the resonant frequencies is not as simple as in the tube closed at both ends. Recall that in a tube closed at both ends resonant frequencies occur at multiples of the lowest resonance; that is, the second resonant frequency is twice the first resonant frequency, and so on. Here, by contrast, the second resonant frequency of a tube that is open at one end has a period which is one-third the duration of the first resonance, and hence the second resonant frequency is three times the first resonant frequency. The general pattern is that the resonant frequencies of a tube closed at one end and open at the other are odd multiples of the first resonance: the second resonance is three times the first, the third is five times the first, and so on. We can write the relationship between resonance number and odd multiples as $(2n - 1)$, where n is the number of the resonant frequency. The second resonance is $(4 - 1)$ multiples of the first, the third resonance is $(6 - 1)$ multiples of the first, and so on.

To summarize, we can model the acoustic properties of the vocal tract during schwa as a tube that is closed at one end (the glottis) and open at the other (the lips). The natural resonances of such a tube meet a couple of boundary conditions comparable to the boundary conditions for the harmonics of a string. The boundary conditions for the resonant frequencies of the tube result from the fact that sound waves are pressure fluctuations moving through space, and therefore the distance it takes to complete one cycle of a wave (its wavelength) can be measured in inches or millimeters. So in standing waves there are points in space where pressure is at a maximum, and others where pressure is at a minimum. The resonances of a tube that is closed at one end have wavelengths such that points of maximum pressure (peaks and valleys) in the standing waves occur at the closed end of the tube, while points of zero pressure occur at the open end. These boundary conditions for resonant frequencies are determined by the compatibility of the sound wave with the tube. Just as the vibration of a guitar string is limited by the fact that the string must be stationary at both ends (figure 5.3), so the resonances of the vocal tract are limited by the nature of the acoustic reflection properties at either end of the vocal tract. The closed end of the tube is compatible with high pressure, the open end with zero pressure. Figure 5.10 illustrates the relative wavelengths of the first three resonances, called vowel "formants," of the vocal tract in

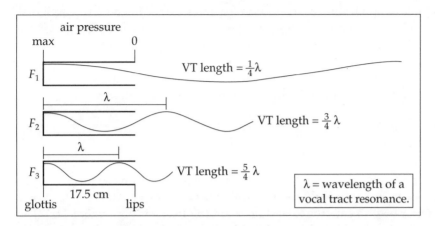

Figure 5.10   The three lowest-frequency pressure waves that meet the boundary conditions for resonating, in an unconstricted vocal tract as in the vowel [ə]. They are labeled F_1–F_3 for vowel "formants" 1–3.

schwa. These sound waves fit into the vocal tract in such a way that there is a pressure maximum at the glottis and a pressure minimum at the lips.

In figure 5.10 standing waves are represented as sine waves in a tube. Maximum pressure at the glottis is indicated when the sine wave is at a peak, zero pressure when the sine wave is midway between a peak and a valley. The lowest resonant frequency has a wavelength that is four times the length of the tube. This is the one labeled F_1 in the figure. Like all the other vocal tract resonances, this standing wave has maximum pressure at the glottis and zero pressure at the lips. You can imagine stretching or compressing the waves in figure 5.10 like springs. The lengths that are shown in the figure are selected out of all possible wavelengths because they meet the boundary conditions for resonance in the vocal tract. Because the frequency of the sound wave is equal to the speed of sound divided by the wavelength ($f = c/\lambda$), and because the wavelengths of the resonances of a tube that is open at one end and closed at the other can be calculated if you know the length of the tube, we can calculate the resonant frequencies of a uniform tube that is closed at one end and open at the other if we know its length. The equations given as (5.2) below derive the first three resonances from the length of the tube.

$$F_1 = c/\lambda_1 = c/(4L) = c/4L$$
$$F_2 = c/\lambda_2 = c/(4/3L) = 3c/4L \qquad (5.2)$$
$$F_3 = c/\lambda_3 = c/(4/5L) = 5c/4L$$

The first expression of each of these resonant frequencies is in terms of the wavelength of the standing wave in the vocal tract. The second defines the standing wave's wavelength in terms of the length of the vocal tract, and the last expression is an algebraic simplification of the second (each resonance has a wavelength that is an odd multiple of the speed of sound divided by four times the length of the vocal tract). These last expressions of the resonant frequencies of a tube that is open at one end and closed at the other can be summarized as in equation (5.3), where n is the number of the resonance (the formant), c is the speed of sound in warm, moist air (35,000 cm/sec), and L is the length of the tube in cm.

$$F_n = \frac{(2n - 1)c}{4L} \tag{5.3}$$

So, for a particular male vocal tract with a length of 17.5 cm the lowest resonant frequency is 35,000 cm/sec divided by 4 times 17.5 cm, or 500 Hz. If the vocal tract is shorter (say 15 cm), the lowest resonant frequency is higher (583 Hz). The second vocal tract resonance is calculated by multiplying the speed of sound by 3 and then dividing by $4L$. For a 17.5 cm vocal tract this comes to 1,500 Hz, and for a 15 cm vocal tract the second resonance is 1,750 Hz. The resonant frequencies of the vocal tract are also called **formants**, and are labeled F_1, F_2, F_3, etc., starting from the lowest resonant frequency.

Cross-modes and straight tubes

Modeling the vocal tract as a straight tube with a sound wave traveling through it lengthwise raises a couple of questions. What happens when the tube has a bend in it (as the vocal tract does)? And why not consider sound waves that resonate in the width of the tube in addition to those that resonate in its length? The answers are "Nothing" and "Sure, why not?"

Sound waves can travel around corners. For example, if you talk into a garden hose, the transmitted sound doesn't change when you bend the hose. Of course, because a garden hose is a long tube, it acts as an acoustic filter, and does alter the sound of your voice; but changing the hose from straight to curved doesn't alter the signal any further. The pressure fluctuations that are sound waves expand spherically from the sound source. The walls of the tube impede this pattern of propagation, but if the tube curves, a sound wave's natural tendency to expand equally in all directions makes it possible for it to turn corners.

Does the width of the tube give rise to resonances comparable to the resonances along the length of the tube that we have been focusing on? The answer is "Yes," but these "cross-modes" are generally so high in frequency that they have no real bearing on the acoustic properties of speech (particularly vowels). For example, consider the wavelength of a resonance traveling up and down (rather than to and fro) in the tube illustrated in figure 5.7. The lowest resonance would have a very short wavelength (twice the width of the tube) and hence a very high frequency. These cross-mode resonances no doubt exist in speech sounds, but have such high frequencies, that for all practical purposes they can be ignored.

Look once again at the power spectrum in figure 5.6. This spectrum shows the acoustic output typical of a vocal tract that has no constrictions (uniform diameter), a length of 17.5 cm, and vocal cord vibration that has a fundamental frequency of 150 Hz. The vocal tract resonances cause peaks in the spectrum to occur at 500 Hz, 1,500 Hz, 2,500 Hz and 3,500 Hz. As the spectrum shows, vocal tract resonances enhance the harmonics with frequencies near the resonant frequencies and damp the other harmonics. Harmonics with frequencies that do not match the resonant frequencies are still present in the signal, but they are relatively weaker as a result of the filtering action of the vocal tract.

In this section we have considered the filtering action of the vocal tract when there are no constrictions in it, in the vowel schwa [ə]. As we have seen, the resonant frequencies of the vocal tract (the formants) are determined by vocal tract length. Consequently, all else being equal, people with short vocal tracts have higher formants than people with long vocal tracts. Additionally, because lip protrusion and larynx lowering lengthen the vocal tract, all formants have a lower frequency as a result of these maneuvers.

5.5 LPC spectral analysis

We have seen that the overall shape of the spectrum shown in figure 5.6, the spectral envelope, is produced by the vocal tract filtering effect. To measure formant frequencies in vowels, we need to be able to extract the overall spectral shape without showing the detailed harmonic structure (like drawing a line connecting the harmonic peaks). In chapter 2 we discussed two methods for looking at the spectral envelope: zero-padded FFT and linear prediction coding (LPC). This section discusses LPC analysis in more detail (see Markel and Gray, 1976, for a more technical and complete description of LPC analysis).

LPC is used in many speech technology applications, including speech and speaker recognition, speech synthesis, and speech coding and transmission. The method takes a small duration of an acoustic waveform, and estimates the vocal tract resonances. Recall from chapter 2 that LPC uses an auto-correlation technique to find prominent frequency components in the speech spectrum. Unlike auto-correlation pitch tracking, however, the auto-correlation lag durations in LPC are short (less than one glottal period), and therefore, rather than capturing the regularly repeating waveform pattern produced by voicing, LPC auto-correlation captures periodicities in the speech waveform produced by formant resonances.

LPC is called a predictive coding algorithm, because it calculates a small set of "predictor" coefficients in a linear combination of waveform samples. As we will see, these coefficients define a filter which, when certain assumptions are met, approximates the vocal tract filter function. The linear predictive formula predicts the amplitude of any arbitrary waveform sample as a function of a small number of preceding samples. For example, with four coefficients the LPC formula is: $\hat{x}_5 = a_1x_1 + a_2x_2 + a_3x_3 + a_4x_4$, where the as are the LPC coefficients and the xs are waveform samples. So in this example, waveform sample $\hat{x}_5$ is estimated

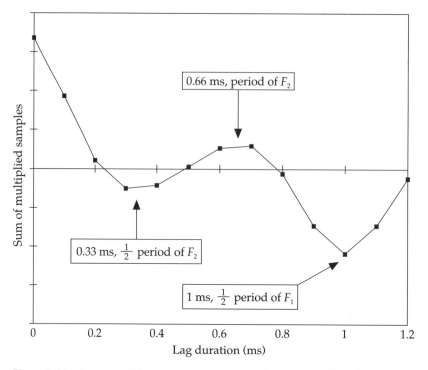

Figure 5.11 Auto-correlation product array produced during an LPC analysis of the waveform shown in figure 5.5. Period durations corresponding to F_1 and F_2 are readily visible in this array as peaks and valleys in the function, while information about the higher formants, although present, is less apparent.

from the values of the four previous samples in the wave-form, and the coefficients (a_i) determine how much weight to put on each of the four samples. Notice how similar the LPC equation is to the equation for digital filters that we discussed in chapter 2 (equation 2.2). The only difference is that in LPC analysis the filter a_i produces an estimate $\hat{x}$ of the input waveform x instead of a newly modified waveform y. When the coefficients are chosen so that the estimation error (the squared difference between the predicted $\hat{x}_5$ and the actual value of x_5) is minimized, they capture the vocal tract filtering characteristics.

To calculate the LPC coefficients, waveform samples from several pitch periods are multiplied by each other at several different lag offsets, using the formula $\sum\limits_{n=0}^{N}\sum\limits_{i=0}^{M} x_n x_{n-i}$ where M is the number of coefficients, N is the number of samples in the analysis window, and i is the lag duration. Figure 5.11 shows the results of this step in the auto-correlation LPC algorithm (with $M = 12$) from the waveform shown in figure 5.5. The arrows in the figure show that the multiplication of waveform samples at different lag durations captures information about the first two formant frequencies as negative values when the lag duration equals half the period, and positive values when the lag duration equals the duration of the

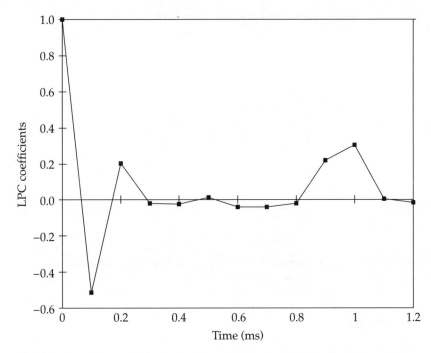

Figure 5.12 LPC coefficients derived from the product array shown in figure 5.11.

period. The largest value occurs when the lag duration equals zero (i.e. when the waveform samples are squared). When the samples in the original waveform separated by some lag i are correlated with each other, the product $x_n x_{n-i}$ is positive; whereas when the lag corresponds to an interval of negative correlation, the product is negative.

Next the set of predictor coefficients, a_i, is calculated. The coefficients retain the frequency information that is captured in the auto-correlation analysis, but the information is expressed as a linear filter function. Figure 5.12 shows the LPC coefficients derived from the product array shown in figure 5.11. As before, there is a large component at 1 ms, which corresponds to half the duration of the period of F_1, but the other formant values are not so readily apparent in the set of coefficients. However, recall that it is often difficult to see the frequency components of a complex wave by visual inspection of the waveform alone, as is certainly the case here.

When we look at a zero-padded FFT of the LPC coefficients (see figure 5.13), it is apparent that LPC analysis captures information about the vocal tract filter function. The LPC spectrum shows the global shape of the spectrum regardless of the specific frequencies of the harmonics, and thus provides an accurate representation of the vocal tract filter function. That is, the peaks in the LPC spectrum correspond to the resonant frequencies of the vocal tract (in this case: 500 Hz, 1,500 Hz, 2,500 Hz, and 3,500 Hz).

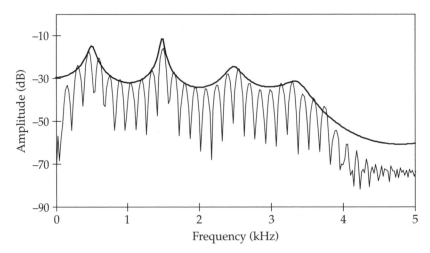

Figure 5.13   FFT and LPC spectra of the vowel [ə]. The acoustic waveform of this vowel was shown in figure 5.5, and the FFT spectrum in figure 5.6. The LPC spectrum (heavy line), which was produced by taking a (zero-padded) FFT of the LPC coefficients shown in figure 5.12, highlights the broad spectral peaks of the vowel (the formant peaks) without regard to the specific frequencies of the harmonics.

LPC is a very useful tool in acoustic phonetics, but it does have some limitations related to the simplifying assumptions used in calculating the vocal tract filter function. First, LPC analysis assumes that the voicing spectrum is primarily shaped by broad spectral peaks with no prominent spectral valleys (anti-formants, see chapter 9). This means that the method is well suited for (nonnasalized) vowels, but will incompletely represent the spectra of speech sounds such as nasals, laterals, and some fricatives, in which spectral valleys are important. Second, it is necessary to specify in advance the number of peaks to find in the spectrum. If the number of anticipated peaks is larger than the number of actual peaks, LPC analysis will posit small (i.e. wide bandwidth) peaks where none actually exist. And if too few peaks are anticipated, LPC will fail to register peaks that actually exist in the spectrum. The number of spectral peaks that LPC analysis will fit to the spectrum is specified by the number of coefficients in the linear predictive equation. Each formant is represented by two coefficients (recall the discussion in chapter 2 of the Nyquist frequency – at least two points are needed to minimally represent a sine wave), with an additional two coefficients being used to capture the overall tilt of the spectrum. Thus, if you anticipate that there will be 10 formants within the frequency range being analyzed, the number of coefficients should be 22 (= (10 × 2) + 2). In practice, the number of formants expected depends on the frequency range being analyzed (which in turn is determined by the sampling rate) and the length of the speaker's vocal tract.

Exercises

Sufficient jargon

Define the following terms: voicing, fundamental frequency of voicing, harmonics, quantal region, nonlinear, resonant frequencies, standing wave, node, antinode, simple harmonic system, wavelength, speed of sound (in cm/sec), acoustic reflection, polarity change, formant, F_1, F_2, F_3, spectral envelope, predictor coefficients.

Short-answer questions

1 Measure the spectral tilt in the spectrum in figure 5.2. Draw a straight line that fits (as closely as possible) the peaks of the harmonics. No straight line will connect all the points exactly, but try to make the sum of the absolute distances between the peaks and the line as small as possible (by the way, this is called "linear regression"). Now measure the amplitude of the line at 1 kHz and at 2 kHz. The spectral tilt is the slope of the line expressed as amount of change per 1 kHz.
2 Calculate the first three resonant frequencies of a tube closed at both ends for each of the following tube lengths: 4 cm, 10 cm, 12 cm.
3 Calculate the first three resonant frequencies of a tube closed at one end and open at the other for each of the following tube lengths: 12 cm, 15 cm, 18 cm.
4 Assuming that lip rounding adds 1 cm to the lengths of each of the tubes mentioned in question 3, does it produce the same frequency change (in Hz) for each of the formants? Does it produce the same frequency change (in Hz) for the F_2 of each of the vocal tract lengths?

CHAPTER 6

Vowels

6.1   Tube models of vowel production

The source-filter theory makes it possible to predict the resonant frequencies of the vocal tract (the formant values) if the cross-sectional area is uniform, as in schwa. Additionally, there are a couple of articulations that alter the overall length of the vocal tract (lip protrusion and larynx lowering) for which this analysis is relevant. However, in order to account for the acoustic properties of other vowels, it is necessary to extend the theory to include vocal tract configurations that involve constrictions.

One way of modeling the acoustic effects of constrictions in vowels is to think of the vocal tract as a *set* of tubes rather than as a single tube (Fant, 1960). This section describes a couple of **tube models** of the vocal tract that can be used to model certain aspects of vowels. The discussion builds on ideas developed in chapter 4, in particular the fact that the resonant frequencies of a tube can be calculated from its length.

An example of a tube model appropriate for some vocal tract configurations is shown in figure 6.1 (the discussion in this section follows Stevens, 1989). In this model, the vocal tract is divided into two tubes. If, as in the figure, the back tube has a cross-sectional area, A_b, that is very much smaller than the cross-sectional area of the front tube, A_f, we can consider the back tube to be closed at the glottis and open at the junction with the front tube; we can also consider the front tube to be closed at the junction with the back tube and open at the other end, which corresponds to the lips. Therefore, because both tubes are closed at one end and open at the other, we can use the vocal tract resonances formula ($F_n = (2n - 1)c/4L$) to calculate the resonances of the front and back tubes (or cavities) separately from their lengths, l_b and l_f. So the resonances of the back cavity are: $F_{bn} = (2n - 1)c/4l_b$, and the resonances of the front cavity are: $F_{fn} = (2n - 1)c/4l_f$.

Source-filter theory party tricks

You can use the source-filter theory to calculate the length of your vocal tract, or, if you want to, the speed of sound in helium.

From the source-filter theory we know that the formant frequencies in schwa can be calculated given the length of the vocal tract. Therefore, if you know the formant values, you should be able to estimate the length of the vocal tract. As a first approximation, the first vowel in *ahead* is produced with a nearly constrictionless (neutral) vocal tract; but the exact vowel quality of the neutral vocal tract varies from person to person, so it might be worthwhile to experiment a bit and see what your neutral vocal tract vowel sounds like. To do this, you need to make spectrograms of a variety of vowel sounds, usually with a quality somewhere between [ə] and [æ], and note the frequency values of the formants (in this chapter we will discuss how different vocal tract shapes result in different formant values). You will know that your vocal tract has a nearly uniform cross-sectional area, the neutral vocal tract shape, when the formants are evenly spaced – that is, when the interval between F_1 and F_2 is the same as the interval between F_2 and F_3, and so on.

So, now that you have found your neutral vocal tract vowel, you can calculate the length of your vocal tract. Take the formula for formants ($F_n = (2n - 1)c/4L$) and put L on the left side ($L = (2n - 1)c/4F_n$). For instance, F_3 in my neutral vowel is 2,600 Hz, so my vocal tract is about 16.8 cm long. I was once asked by a TV reporter (who was rather proud of his smooth speaking voice), "What does this spectrogram tell you about the difference between your voice and mine?" He was surprised when I told him that the spectrogram showed that his vocal tract was smaller than mine. I never suspected that he might be a little sensitive about his height.

When a person inhales helium and then speaks, the vocal tract's resonant frequencies increase (and hence the person sounds funny). This is not due to a change in the length of the vocal tract, needless to say, but rather to a change in the acoustic medium (helium versus air), and consequently the speed of sound. So if you know the length of a person's vocal tract, you should be able to find the speed of sound in helium by measuring the formants in schwa produced on a breath of helium. For example, when I produce speech while breathing a mystery gas, the F_3 in my schwa is 1,960 Hz. So, using a version of the formants formula ($c = F_n 4L/(2n - 1)$), we can calculate the speed of sound in the mystery gas. It is 26,300 cm/sec. If you want to know what the gas is, look it up.

The resonant frequencies produced by this model with different front and back cavity lengths (where the overall length of the vocal tract was kept at 16 cm) are shown in figure 6.2. In this **nomogram**, an articulatory parameter is shown on the horizontal axis, and the acoustic output of the vocal tract is shown on the vertical axis. The parameter that is shown on the horizontal axis of figure 6.2 is the length of the back cavity in cm, and the resonant frequencies of the tube model are

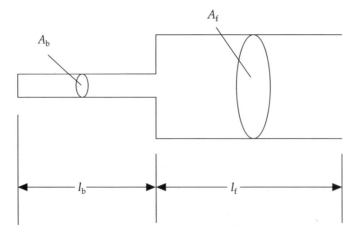

Figure 6.1   A two-tube model of the vocal tract that approximates the shape of the vocal tract for [ɑ].

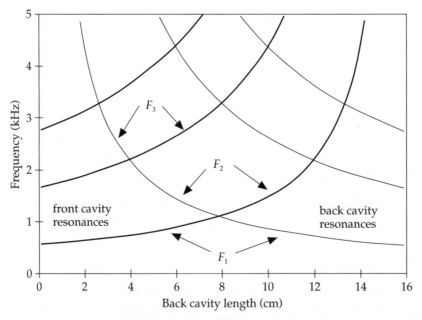

Figure 6.2   Natural resonant frequencies of the back tube (light lines) and front tube (heavy lines) in the tube model shown in figure 6.1 for different lengths of the back cavity. Overall vocal tract length is 16 cm, so the front cavity length is 16 cm minus the back cavity length.

shown on the vertical axis. When the back cavity is very short, its resonant frequencies are very high, so the lowest resonances of the vocal tract are affiliated with the front cavity (in the case where $l_b = 0$, the model is the same as the single uniform tube model we discussed in the previous chapter). When the back cavity is a little over 4 cm long, its lowest resonance is lower than the second resonance

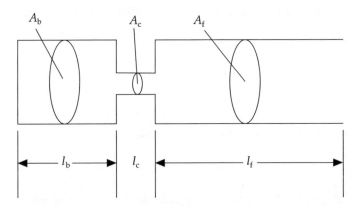

Figure 6.3 Tube model of vocal tract configurations that have a short constriction at some point in the vocal tract.

of the front cavity. So, when the back cavity is between 4 and 8 cm long, the lowest resonance of the tube model (F_1) is a resonance of the front cavity, while the second resonance (F_2) is a resonance of the back cavity. When the length of the back cavity equals the length of the front cavity ($l_b = l_f = 8$ cm), both tubes have the same resonant frequencies. In a two-tube system such as this the front and back resonances are not realized with the same frequency, because our initial assumption that the back tube is open at one end and that the front tube is closed at one end is not strictly true. Depending on their relative cross-sectional areas (A_b and A_f), the two tubes are acoustically coupled with each other, and when the resonant frequencies of the two tubes would be theoretically about the same, they diverge slightly from the values predicted for the uncoupled tubes. (Acoustic coupling is discussed further in chapter 7.) With acoustic coupling the F_1 value when $l_b = l_f$ is about 750 Hz, and the F_2 value about 1,250 Hz. The exact effect of acoustic coupling depends on the cross-sectional areas of the two tubes, and it occurs whenever the frequencies of the front and back cavity resonances converge.

The tube model shown in figure 6.1 (with the length of the back cavity about the same as the length of the front cavity, and with a back cavity cross-sectional area that is much smaller than the cross-sectional area of the front cavity) is a reasonable (albeit oversimplified) model of the vocal tract shape for /ɑ/. Using the two-tube model in figure 6.1, we correctly predict that /ɑ/ has a high F_1 frequency and a low F_2 frequency relative to the F_1 and F_2 is schwa.

Figure 6.3 shows another type of tube model of the vocal tract. In this case a constriction separates the front tube from the back tube. As before, we can calculate the resonant frequencies of the front and back tubes separately, using formulas like the one used to calculate the resonances of a uniform tube. The resonances of the front tube are calculated using the formula for resonances of a tube closed at one end (the constriction) and open at the other (the lips). The resonances of the back tube are calculated using the formula for a tube that is closed at both ends (equation 6.1 below) because the back tube is effectively closed at both ends.

Recall from chapter 4 that this formula, like the one for a tube open at one end, derives the resonant frequency from the length of the tube, and the resonant frequencies increase as the length of the tube decreases.

$$F_n = \frac{nc}{2L}$$ (6.1)

where n is the number of the resonance, c is the speed of sound (35,000 cm/sec), and L is the length of the tube (l_b).

In addition to resonances of the front and back cavities, in the vocal tract configuration shown in figure 6.3, the back tube and the constriction form a resonant system called a "Helmholtz resonator," in which the volume of air in the constriction oscillates like a piston in and out of the constriction. The noise produced when you blow across the top of a beer (or soft-drink) bottle is the result of Helmholtz resonance (with turbulence as the sound source). The neck of the bottle is analogous to the constriction, and the body of the bottle is analogous to the back cavity of the vocal tract. The natural resonant frequency of this Helmholtz resonator is determined by the relative volumes of air in the back cavity and in the constriction, and can be calculated by equation (6.2).

$$f = \frac{c}{2\pi} \sqrt{\frac{A_c}{A_b l_b l_c}}$$ (6.2)

The acoustic output of the tube model is shown in figure 6.4. In calculating the formant values for this nomogram, the overall length of the model vocal tract was fixed as before at 16 cm, the length of the constriction was 2 cm, and the length of the front tube was dependent on the length of the back tube ($l_f = 16 - 2 - l_b$). The nomogram (figure 6.4) shows the resonant frequencies of the vocal tract for a range of constriction locations (some of which are not humanly possible), extending from the glottis to the lips. As discussed in connection with figure 6.2, when the front and back tubes are acoustically coupled, the resonant frequencies do not actually intersect (e.g. F_2 when $l_b = 10$ cm). The first formant (dashed line), which is the Helmholtz resonance, varies as a function of the length of the back cavity.

To understand what you are looking at in figure 6.4, remember that the resonant frequencies of a uniform tube depend on the length of the tube. Short tubes have higher resonant frequencies than long tubes. So, looking at the frequency values of F_2, we see that when the constriction is located between 3 and 10 cm from the glottis, the second highest resonant frequency in the output of the model (the F_2) is a resonance of the front tube, because when the front tube is long, its resonant frequencies are low, and when the back tube is short, its resonant frequencies are high. As the constriction is moved forward, the back tube gets longer, so its resonant frequencies get lower, and the front tube gets shorter, so its resonant frequencies get higher. When the constriction is a little less than

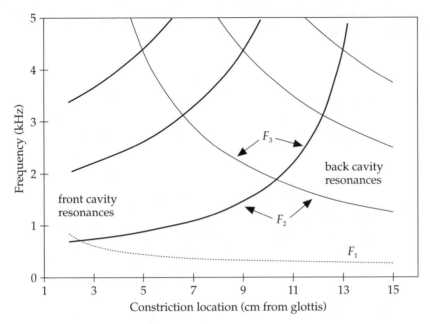

Figure 6.4 Resonant frequencies of the back tube (light lines), front tube (heavy lines) and Helmholtz resonance (dashed line) in the tube model illustrated in figure 6.3. Frequencies are plotted as a function of different back tube lengths (l_b), with the length of the constriction fixed at 2 cm and the total length of the model fixed at 16 cm.

11 cm from the glottis, the cavity affiliation of F_2 switches from front to back. That is, the lowest resonance of the back cavity becomes lower than the lowest resonance of the front cavity. A constriction 11 cm from the glottis in this tube model approximates the vocal tract configuration for the high front vowel [i]. As we will see below, the formant values predicted by the tube model (F_1 = 300 Hz, F_2 = 1,900 Hz, and F_3 = 2,200 Hz) are approximately those found in [i].

6.2   Perturbation theory

There is another way of modeling the acoustic consequences of vocal tract constrictions, commonly called **perturbation theory**. In this approach to modeling vowel acoustics, the relationship between air pressure and velocity plays an important role. (Further discussion of perturbation theory can be found in Chiba and Kajiyama, 1941, and Mrayati et al., 1988.)

Imagine an air molecule oscillating in place as in figure 6.5. At the point where the air particle is crowded next to one of its neighbors, it is in the process of changing direction. Its movement has been slowed down, due to crowding with a neighbor; air pressure is at a maximum, because the air particles are squished together, while the molecule's velocity is at a minimum, because it is in the

Figure 6.5 An air molecule oscillating in place. Points of maximum pressure occur when the particle is crowded next to one of its neighbors, while the point of maximum velocity occurs when the particle is equidistant from its neighbors.

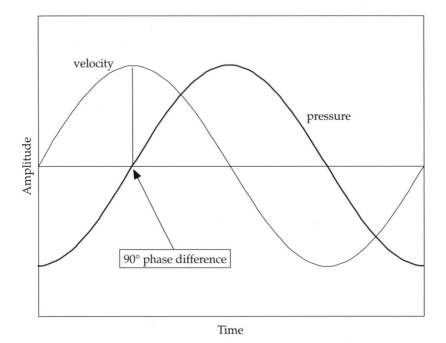

Figure 6.6 The relationship between velocity and pressure. When velocity is at either a positive or a negative maximum, pressure equals zero, and when pressure is at either a positive or a negative maximum, velocity equals zero.

process of changing direction. When the molecule swings back the other way, it reaches a point midway between its neighbors at which crowding (air pressure) is at a minimum while velocity is at a maximum. This relationship between velocity and pressure is shown in figure 6.6. Maxima of velocity correspond to points where pressure equals zero, and maxima of pressure correspond to points where velocity equals zero.

Figure 6.7, which is adapted from Chiba and Kajiyama's (1941) classic study, shows standing waves in the vocal tract (both as a uniform straight tube and in sagittal section). These waveforms show the standing waves in terms of velocity, rather than pressure (as in figures 5.7–5.9). Recall from chapter 5 that the natural resonances of the vocal tract have maximum pressure at the glottis and minimum pressure at the lips. Because of the relationship between pressure and velocity (figure 6.6), the natural resonances also have minimum velocity at the

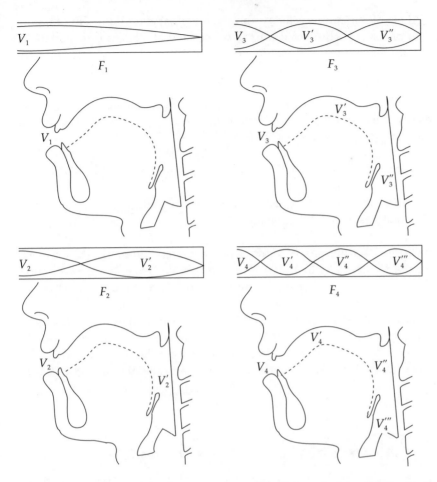

Figure 6.7 Locations of velocity nodes (points of maximum velocity) and antinodes (points of maximum pressure) in a straight tube open at one end and in the unconstricted vocal tract. Points of maximum velocity are labeled V_n (numbered by primes from the front of the vocal tract), and points of maximum pressure are indicated by the intersections of the sine waves in the uniform tube. Velocity nodes and antinodes are shown in separate graphs for each of the first four formants (labeled F_n). After Chiba and Kajiyama, 1941.

glottis and maximum velocity at the lips, as shown in figure 6.7. In figure 6.7, points of maximum velocity are labeled V_n. These are the locations of the velocity **nodes**. The velocity **antinodes** (points of maximum pressure) occur at zero velocity (recall these terms from chapter 5). Velocity waves for the four lowest resonant frequencies of a uniform tube closed at one end are shown in separate pairs of tube and vocal tract illustrations labeled F_n. The top diagram in each pair shows a uniform tube, and the bottom of each pair shows the approximate locations of the velocity nodes in a vocal tract.

The **perturbation theory** described by Chiba and Kajiyama relates vocal tract constrictions to formant frequencies by taking into account the kinetic energy present at points of maximum velocity and the potential energy present at points of maximum pressure. If the vocal tract is constricted at a point of high kinetic energy (velocity maximum), air particle movement is impeded, and consequently the frequency of the movement decreases; while, on the other hand, if the vocal tract is constricted at a point of high potential energy (pressure maximum), air particle movement is enhanced, and consequently the frequency of the movement increases. These effects of constrictions on vocal tract resonant frequencies can be summarized by two rules of thumb:

1   Constriction of the vocal tract near a point of maximum velocity (labeled V_n) *lowers* the formant frequency.
2   Constriction of the vocal tract near a point of maximum pressure (the intersections) *raises* the formant frequency.

The perturbation theory rules of thumb apply separately for each of the formants (i.e. each of the resonances illustrated in figure 6.7). For instance, a constriction in the pharynx falls near a pressure maximum in the F_1 resonance, and thus the perturbation model predicts that the F_1 of [ɑ] is higher than the F_1 found in the neutral (constrictionless) vocal tract configuration. At the same time a constriction in the pharynx falls near a velocity maximum in the F_2 resonance, and thus the model predicts that the F_2 of [ɑ] will be lower than the F_2 produced by the constrictionless vocal tract. So, perturbation theory and the tube model in figure 6.1 give the same result for [ɑ].

Cross-sectional area and vocal tract constriction

Vowel formant frequencies are predicted in perturbation theory by noting deviations from the uniform tube. Intuitively, deviations from a uniform tube are produced by constrictions in the vocal tract. So the perturbation theory rules of thumb are stated in terms of constriction location. It is important to realize that by "constriction," we do not necessarily mean an active vocal tract-narrowing gesture. Rather, constriction in this context means a small cross-sectional area relative to the uniform tube. The area of a cross-section of the vocal tract may be small at a particular point, even though there is no active constriction gesture. The vowel [æ] in the word *ash* is an example. Mid-sagittal X-rays of productions of [æ] consistently show no evidence of any active vocal tract constriction. Nonetheless, both F_1 and F_2 are higher than you would predict, assuming uniform cross-sectional area in the vocal tract. This acoustic pattern is consistent with a vocal tract that has a small crosssectional area just above the larynx (at a minimum velocity point for both F_1 and F_2). This "constriction" in [æ] is just a property of the anatomy of the vocal tract, not the result of an active constriction gesture.

The two models also give the same result for the F_2 of [i]. The nomogram in figure 6.4 shows that F_2 for a constriction 10 cm from the glottis, as in the vowel [i], has an F_2 value close to 2 kHz. This result is consistent with the perturbation theory analysis of the same vocal tract configuration. Looking again at figure 5.7, notice that a constriction in the vocal tract 10 cm from the glottis narrows the vocal tract at the location of a pressure maximum for F_2, and by perturbation theory we therefore expect the frequency of F_2 to be higher than it is in the neutral, unconstricted vocal tract. I will leave it as an exercise for the reader to compare the perturbation theory and tube model predictions for the other formants of [i].

The utility of perturbation theory is nicely illustrated by the third formant (F_3) in American English [ɹ]. This sound, which is produced with three simultaneous vocal tract constrictions (labial, coronal, and pharyngeal), is unlike other vocalic sounds because the F_3 has an unusually low frequency (Lindau, 1985). The vocal tract configuration for American English [ɹ] is more complicated than any that we have seen in a tube model up to this point, but the low F_3 is easy to predict using perturbation theory. Tongue bunching or retroflexion (it doesn't matter which) narrows the vocal tract at point V'_3; lip rounding narrows the tract at point V_3; and pharyngeal constriction narrows the tract a V''_3. Thus, all three of the constrictions in [ɹ] occur near points of maximum velocity in the F_3 standing wave, and therefore perturbation theory correctly predicts that the frequency of F_3 in [ɹ] will be low relative to other vocalic sounds.

The comparisons of perturbation theory and tube models for the vowels [i] and [a] show that perturbation theory and tube models make similar predictions for vowel formant frequencies. However, when there is more than one vocal tract constriction, as in [ɹ], it is easier to apply perturbation theory for a particular vocal tract configuration, while for less complicated vocal tract configurations, it is simpler to derive quantitative predictions of the formant values for a range of articulations, using tube models.

There is another important distinction between perturbation theory and tube models. Tube models assume that vocal tract resonances arise from the resonant properties of particular cavities in the vocal tract. That is, the formant values predicted by tube models are affiliated with one or the other of the tubes. Consequently, the assumptions of tube models are more closely met in articulations that have relatively narrow constrictions, and thus not too much coupling between the tubes. On the other hand, the assumptions of perturbation theory are more closely met by articulations in which the vocal tract is mainly unobstructed.

6.3 "Preferred" vowels – quantal theory and adaptive dispersion

When discussing the quanta in mapping glottal width to acoustic output, the figure that I presented (figure 5.4) was a kind of nomogram. Values of an articulatory parameter, glottal width, were plotted on the horizontal axis, and hypothetical acoustic output was plotted on the vertical axis. Quantal theory predicted that plateaus in the articulatory-to-acoustics mapping for glottal width (regions of stability) would define cross-linguistically preferred glottal articulations. Similarly, Stevens (1989) claims that nomograms such as those in figures 6.2 and 6.4 relating oral vowel articulations to acoustic output can be used to predict some cross-linguistic trends in vowel inventories. He notes that at points in the nomograms where the cavity affiliation of a formant changes (points where front and back cavity resonances intersect), a range of places of articulation may lead to approximately the same acoustic output. For instance, in figure 6.4, when the back cavity is between 10 and 11 cm long, there is a region of stability in F_2; back cavity lengths over a range of about 2 cm result in about the same F_2 value. This observation predicts that the vowel [i], which has a constriction at about 10 cm from the glottis (a palatal constriction) that is acoustically characterized by a high F_2 and not much distance between F_2 and F_3, will be common in the languages of the world. A similar cross-linguistic prediction can be made from the nomogram in figure 6.2. This figure shows an intersection of the lowest front and back cavity resonances when the front and back tubes have about the same length (8 cm in the model). This vocal tract constriction, which is typical of the vowel [ɑ], is acoustically characterized by a relatively high-frequency F_1 and relatively low-frequency F_2. Finally, in nomograms that I have not reproduced, Stevens showed that with lip rounding added to the tube model shown in figure 6.3 there is a region of stability near the soft palate, as in the production of [u].

Quantal theory claims, then, that regions of stability in the mapping between articulation and the frequency of F_2 define as the most acoustically stable vowels (that is, the vowels that have the most room for slop in their productions) the corner vowels [i], [ɑ], and [u]. These are also the vowels that occur most frequently in the languages of the world (Maddieson, 1984).

Lindblom's (1990) theory of adaptive dispersion offers a different explanation for the cross-linguistic preference for the corner vowels. In the adaptive dispersion view, the corner vowels are most common in the languages of the world precisely because they are the corner vowels. That is, given the range of possible F_1 and F_2 values that can be produced in vowels, the vowels that can be most reliably distinguished from each other are those that are maximally distinct. So, if we assume that listeners' abilities to hear vowel distinctions provide a selectional pressure on segment inventories (in the diachronic development of language), we would predict that the most common vowels in the languages of the world would be the ones that have extreme formant values (see section 6.5). Adaptive dispersion is a theory about stability in communication, taking into account the role of the listener; while quantal theory is about stability in only one aspect of communication, the articulation-to-acoustics mapping. Although adaptive dispersion makes predictions about preferred vowels, the theory has not been extended to other speech sounds. Quantal theory, on the other hand, while focusing on a narrower aspect of speech communication, has been applied to several types of segments.

6.4 Vowel formants and the acoustic vowel space

Figure 6.8 shows spectrograms of a set of words illustrating the plain voiced vowels of Jalapa Mazatec (an Otomanguean language spoken in Oaxaca, Mexico). Glosses are shown below:

[si]   *dirty*
[se]   *he sings*
[sɑ]   *moon*
[so]   *you*
[su]   *lukewarm*

The center frequencies of the first three vowel formants are traced in each vowel. As you can see, the formants are relatively steady during these monophthongs. Additionally, these spectrograms show that vowel distinctions are carried by the frequencies of the first and second formants.

Figure 6.9 shows a plot of average F_1 and F_2 frequencies of each of the five Mazatec vowels in an "acoustic vowel space." Note that the acoustic vowel space is similar to the traditional impressionistic vowel triangle. Vowel height is negatively correlated with F_1 frequency; [high] vowels have low F_1, and [low] vowels have high F_1 (the F_1 axis is plotted with low frequencies at the top to emphasize the correlation between impressionistic vowel height and F_1 frequency). Similarly, vowel frontness is correlated with F_2; [front] vowels have high F_2, and [back] vowels have low F_2. These acoustic correlates of vowel features have been noted for centuries, and were especially apparent when the sound spectrograph was developed (Joos, 1948). It has been suggested that the distinctive features of vowels are tied to these acoustic properties, rather than to articulatory properties, because there are individual differences in vowel articulation and inconsistencies between patterns of linguistic vowel "height" and "frontness" and measured tongue height and frontness during vowel production (Johnson et al., 1993; Ladefoged et al., 1972) and between measured muscular tension and linguistic "tenseness" (Raphael and Bell-Berti, 1975; see also Lindau, 1978, 1979; Halle and Stevens, 1969; Perkell, 1971; Stockwell, 1973).

6.5 Auditory and acoustic representations of vowels

The auditory characteristics of vowels are different from their acoustic representations – seen in spectrograms and predicted by the source-filter theory of speech – because of the nonlinearities in the auditory system that we discussed in chapter 3 (see Liljencrants and Lindblom, 1972; Syrdal and Gophal, 1986; Miller, 1989; Traunmüller, 1981, for further discussion of the auditory representation of vowels).

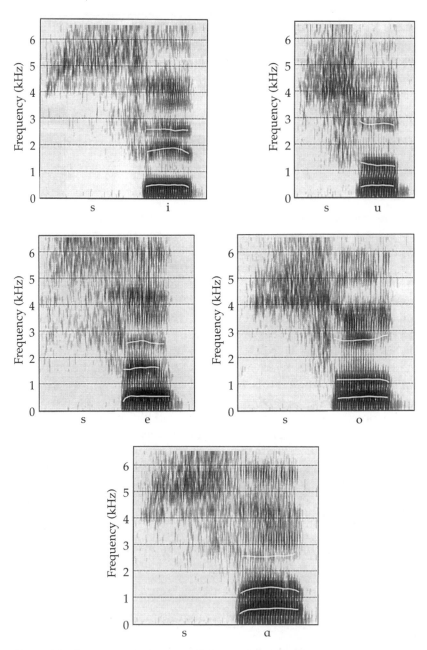

Figure 6.8 Spectrograms of the Jalapa Mazatec words listed in the text, as produced by a male speaker. IPA transcriptions of the words are given below each spectrogram.

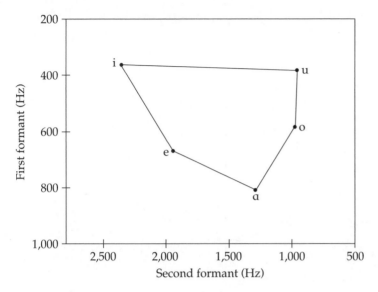

Figure 6.9 The acoustic vowel space of the plain voiced vowels of Jalapa Mazatec. Average of four male speakers.

Figure 6.10 illustrates some differences between acoustic and auditory spectra: (a) shows LPC spectra of the five vowels of Mazatec shown in figure 6.8, and (b) shows auditory spectra of the same vowels. These auditory spectra were produced from the same acoustic waveform windows that were used to produce the LPC spectra by a computerized simulation of the peripheral auditory system (section 3.4). I have drawn lines connecting the first two formants in each vowel, and in the auditory spectra an additional line connecting the first harmonic of voicing.

The acoustic and auditory spectra are matched for frequency range (0–10 kHz in both), so the differences you see in the types of representation are due to properties of the analysis, not to artifacts of presentation. One of the most striking differences between the auditory and acoustic spectra has to do with the proportion of the display occupied by F_1 and F_2. F_1 and F_2 are confined to the lower quarter of the frequency scale in the acoustic spectra, whereas they take up half the frequency scale in the auditory spectra. Consequently, changes in F_1 or F_2 are easily noted in the auditory spectra, while they remain somewhat obscure in the LPC spectra. This difference corresponds to the observation that much of the information used in speech communication is present at frequencies below 2,000 Hz (Miller and Nicely, 1955).

Another of the differences between the auditory and acoustic vowel spectra in figure 6.10 is that the first harmonic (F_0) is resolved in the auditory spectra, but not in the LPC spectra. Of course, it is possible to calculate FFT spectra in which the F_0 is resolved in an acoustic representation, but then the formant peaks are not well defined. Auditory spectra are interesting, because auditory critical bands have a narrow enough bandwidth at low frequencies to resolve the first harmonic as a separate peak, while the critical bands at higher frequencies have broad

(a)

(b)

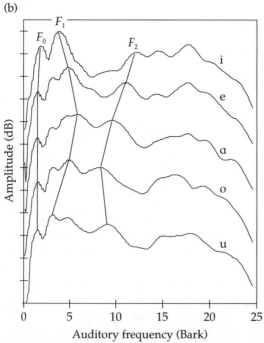

Figure 6.10 Acoustic and auditory spectra of the vowel sounds shown in figure 6.8: (a) LPC spectra taken from the middle of the vowel; (b) auditory spectra of the same acoustic waveform window. The interval between ticks on the vertical axis in both panels is 20 dB. Window size for both the LPC and auditory spectrum was 20 ms.

enough bandwidths to smear together adjacent harmonics into formant peaks. So the nonlinear frequency response of the auditory system enhances the relative importance of the F_1/F_2 region, while the widths of the critical bands tend to smear together harmonics in the formant peaks.

6.6   Cross-linguistic vowel perception

Figure 6.11 shows perceptual spaces drawn from Terbeek's (1977) cross-linguistic study of vowel perception. Terbeek used naturally produced monophthongal vowel sounds in the context [bəb_], that he produced himself. He used a really interesting method to measure perceptual distance. He presented the vowels in triads and asked listeners to judge which of the two vowels are more similar to each other and which two are most different from each other. So, for example, the listener might hear:

A	B	C
bəbi	bəby	bəbu

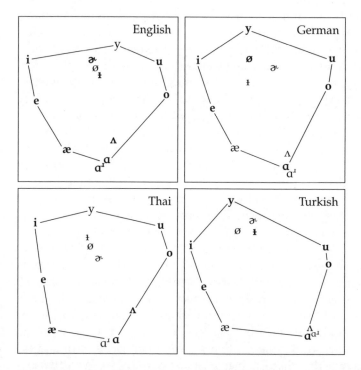

Figure 6.11   Perceptual vowel spaces for listeners who speak English, German, Thai, and Turkish. The spaces were computed from Terbeek's (1977) dissimilarity matrices (Appendix I). I scaled the spaces using the regression coefficient relating raw dissimilarity and normalized distance in the MDS solutions, and I rotated the vowel spaces so that the line connecting [i] and [u] is horizontal. Vowels plotted with non-bold face symbols do not occur in the language (for example English has no /y/ phoneme).

and decide that [i] and [u] are the most different and that [y] and [u] are the most similar. Terbeek then tallied a "dissimilarity matrix" of the number of times that a particular pair was judged to be more different than another pair.

I took Terbeek's dissimilarity matrices for listeners from four different languages and made the perceptual maps that you see in figure 6.11. There are lots of interesting things to notice in these displays, but we'll just look at four general observations about vowel perception here.

First, notice how similar these perceptual vowel spaces are to the acoustic vowel space in figure 6.9. This is remarkable because the perceptual spaces are built from listener's judgements of similarity and disimilarity, while the acoustic space is simply a plot of the F1 and F2 of the vowels. Evidently the formant frequencies matter in vowel perception.

Second, notice how the inventory of distinctive sounds in a language influences perception. To see this compare the German and Turkish spaces with the English and Thai spaces. Both German and Turkish have /y/ as a phoneme, so it is interesting that [y] pulls further away from the other vowels, forming a sort of peak at the top of the space. Similarly, neither German nor Turkish has [ʌ] as a distinctive sound and in both of them, compared with Thai and English, [ʌ] seems to be merged with [ɑ]. If a sound is used distinctively listeners will tend to hear it as more different from other nearby sounds than if it is not used to contrast words in the language.

Third, notice what happens with [æ]. Even though this particular sound is not distinctively present in German and Turkish, these listeners keep [æ] distinct from [e] and [ɑ] just as do English and Thai listeners for whom [æ] is a phoneme. This observation seems to suggest that raw acoustic/auditory distinctiveness matters in all languages. [ʌ] may fall together with [ɑ] because they are auditorily similar, but [æ] is distinct enough to resist merger with other vowel sounds.

Finally, notice how the geometry of the perceptual space changes from language to language. These are the same exact acoustic signals being heard by listeners who have different linguistic backgrounds, so it is interesting that for English speakers the high front round vowel [y] is closer to the high back round vowel [u], while for German and Turkish [y] is more similar to the high front unrounded vowel [i]. This cross-linguistic difference may relate to how American English [u] is pronounced – namely that we tend to front it so that it is like the high central rounded vowel [ʉ] or even centralized and unrounded like [ɨ]. Both of these realizations result in a higher second formant frequency, such as the one found in [y]. So, even though Terbeek's [u] may have had a low F2 frequency, for English speakers it represents a vowel category that can also have a higher F2 frequency and thus [y] is more similar to [u] than it is to [i]. For German and Turkish speakers it may be that the perception of [y] evokes the front tongue position of [i] so that the relatively greater similarity of [i] and [y] reflects articulatory knowledge that English speakers don't have. We can see a similar sort of language specific perceptual organization in the relative backness of [ɑ] in Turkish versus the more central location of [ɑ] in the other languages. It may be that the presence of a backness vowel harmony rule in Turkish emphasizes to Turkish speakers a linguistic affinity of [ɑ] and other [back] vowels that is not highlighted by the phonologies of the other languages in this study.

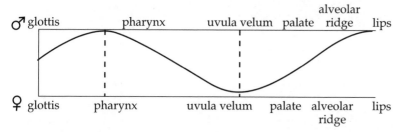

Figure 6.12   Standing wave of the third formant resonance (in a tube that is open at one end and closed at the other), with articulatory landmarks for typical male and female speakers identified. From Hagiwara, 1995, p. 12; reprinted with permission.

Exercises

Sufficient jargon

Define the following terms: source-filter theory, tube model, nomogram, Helmholtz resonator, perturbation theory, node (in terms of both velocity and pressure), antinode (in terms of both velocity and pressure), cross-sectional area, adaptive dispersion, [high] vowels (in terms of F_1), [low] vowels (in terms of F_1), [front] vowels (in terms of F_2), [back] vowels (in terms of F_2).

Short-answer questions

1   Referring to figures 6.1 and 6.2, what are the frequencies of F_1 and F_2 when the back cavity is 5 cm long? Is F_1 a front cavity resonance or a back cavity resonance? What are F_1 and F_2 (and their cavity affiliations) when the front cavity is 5 cm long?
2   According to equation 6.2, constriction area (A_c) plays a role in F_1 frequency. Verify this by calculating F_1 for vocal tracts with these parameters: $A_b = 3$ cm^2, $l_b = 4$ cm, $l_c = 2$ cm, and with areas of constriction that range from $A_c = 0.05$ cm^2 to $A_c = 0.2$ cm^2. What is the frequency of F_1 when $A_c = 0$ cm^2?
3   Figure 6.12 shows the F_3 standing wave with articulatory land-marks for typical male and female speakers. Using perturbation theory, describe the articulations that will produce the lowest F_3 in [ɹ]. How do these "best" articulations differ for men and women?
4   Measure the frequencies of the first and second formants at the midpoints of the Mazatec vowels shown in figure 6.8 and plot them with the average values shown in figure 6.9. How is the speaker who produced the words shown in figure 6.8 different from the average? Is there evidence in this comparison that his vocal tract is longer or shorter than average? Is there evidence that his speaking style or rate differed from the others?
5   What does a diphthong look like in the acoustic vowel space? Measure the formant values of the diphthong shown in figure 3.8 at four or five equally spaced points in time, and plot the values (connected by a line) in an acoustic vowel space. The theory of adaptive dispersion (and perhaps also quantal theory) assumes that vowel categories are kept distinct by having different locations in the acoustic vowel space. How do diphthongs complicate theories of "preferred" vowels?
6   What is the small peak between F_0 and F_1 in [e], [ɑ], and [o] in figure 6.10b? Why does this peak show up in these spectra? And how is this aspect of auditory spectra likely to make it difficult to find F_1 in cochleagrams?

CHAPTER 7

Fricatives

The acoustic theory of speech production, in addition to offering a theoretical description of vowel acoustics, provides an account of the acoustic properties of fricatives. The *source* of noise (acoustic energy) in fricatives is turbulent airflow which is produced as air escapes from a narrow constriction somewhere in the vocal tract. This aperiodic noise is filtered by the vocal tract. This chapter describes the turbulent noise source and vocal tract filtering in fricatives, then some quantal aspects of the articulation-to-acoustics mapping in fricative production; and a comparison of auditory and acoustic properties of fricatives is presented. The chapter ends with a section on fricative perception.

7.1 Turbulence

When you blow through a straw, it makes an aperiodic hissing noise. This noise is the acoustic consequence of irregular air molecule motions that are produced when air exits a relatively narrow channel. When fast-moving air in the channel hits inert outside air, the airstream becomes chaotic (the main area of noise generation is within eight diameters of the end of the straw). The main factors that determine whether airflow is turbulent or not are the size of the channel and the volume velocity of the airflow (volume of air going past a certain point per unit time). For instance, if 100 cm^3 per second of air flows through a channel, turbulent airflow is created if the channel area is less than 10 mm^2, but not if the channel area is 20 mm^2. So, you can get turbulent airflow more easily from a narrow straw than a wide one.

Because the motions of air molecules in turbulent airflow are irregular, the sound pressure waves associated with turbulent airflow are random, like those

The aerodynamics of freeways and fricatives

The behavior of cars on a freeway provides useful analogies for several aerodynamic properties of fricatives.

Particle velocity, the speed of air particles, is like the speed of a car shown on the speedometer. *Volume velocity*, the number of air particles passing a point, is like the count produced by one of those car-counting things you run over, which measures the number of cars per unit time crossing a particular place.

Laminal flow occurs when all the cars stay in their lanes, and move smoothly down the freeway. *Turbulent flow* occurs when cars change lanes a lot; there is some random side-to-side motion in addition to the forward movement.

Channel turbulence on the freeway can occur when the highway widens from two lanes to six. Cars shoot out of the narrow passage and change lanes when the road widens. *Obstacle turbulence* is like the lane changing that occurs when a car is stalled on the freeway. Cars change lanes to move around the obstacle.

Aerodynamic impedance, the resistance of a channel to airflow, is seen in the difference between two-lane and four-lane roads. Larger channels are generally capable of greater volume velocity than narrow channels. That is, larger channels impede flow less.

If volume velocity remains constant, particle velocity increases as channel width decreases. When the number of lanes goes from four to two, there is a big slow-down just before the change, and then cars go faster once they get into the narrow part. In order for the same number of cars to pass through the narrow part as through the wide part (equal volume velocity), the cars have to go faster in the narrow part (higher particle velocity).

of white noise. However, unlike white noise, the spectrum of turbulent noise normally seen in fricatives is not completely flat. As figure 7.1 shows, the spectrum above 1,000 Hz has gradually decreasing amplitude with increasing frequency.

This type of noise occurs in fricatives and in most voiceless sounds. For example, in [h] turbulence is created when air from the lungs passes through the glottis, because the passage between the vocal folds is relatively narrow, and the rate of airflow is relatively high. (The rate of airflow is quite high in aspiration, as you can tell by comparing how long you can sustain [h] versus [a].) So the main difference between the [h] and the vowel in the word *heed* is that the sound source in [h] is aperiodic turbulent noise produced at the glottis, whereas the sound source in [i] is a complex periodic wave (voicing). Both the vowel and the [h] have formant values, which are due to the filtering action of the vocal tract (although in [h], more than vowels, the trachea also contributes to the acoustic filtering of the sound source). Other fricatives also have acoustic energy in specific vocal tract resonances, but before we discuss the place of articulation in fricatives, there are two other points to be made about turbulent noise.

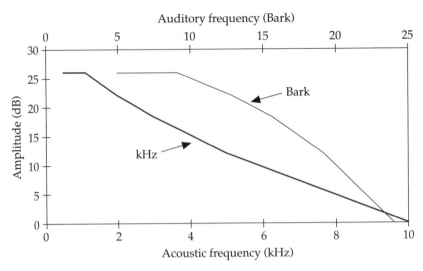

Figure 7.1 Power spectrum of turbulent noise (see Shadle, 1985). The heavy line shows the spectrum in kHz, and the light line shows the same spectrum on the Bark frequency scale.

First, the amplitude of turbulent noise is determined by the velocity of the air molecules as they pass through a channel. (This refers to particle velocity; see "the aerodynamics of freeways" box above.) The faster the air molecules move, the louder the sound. Since particle velocity is related to channel area, it is also true that, for a given rate of airflow out of the mouth (volume velocity), the narrower the channel, the louder the turbulent noise. This is illustrated in figure 7.2a, where the amplitude of the fricative noise is shown on the vertical axis, and the area of the constriction is shown on the horizontal axis. Figure 7.2b shows the same relationship, but with the assumption that air pressure widens the constriction slightly.

Second, in addition to being produced when a jet of air escapes from a narrow channel, turbulent noise is also produced when a jet of air hits a downstream obstacle. An example of such a configuration is shown in figure 7.3. The presence of an obstacle results in increased amplitude of turbulent noise (compare lane changing when a freeway widens and lane changing when a car is blocking a lane), and the noise is generated at the obstacle, rather than at some fixed distance beyond the constriction. It can be argued that almost all fricative noises involve turbulence produced by airflow hitting an obstacle. In [s] and [ʃ] the upper and lower teeth respectively function as turbulence-producing obstacles; but notice that even the amplitude of [f] decreases when you (manually) hold your upper lip up, suggesting that the upper lip functions as an obstacle in the production of the labio-dental fricative. (This may be relevant to Maddieson's (1984) observation that labio-dental fricatives are more common in the languages of the world than are bilabial fricatives, because obstacle turbulence tends to be louder than channel turbulence).

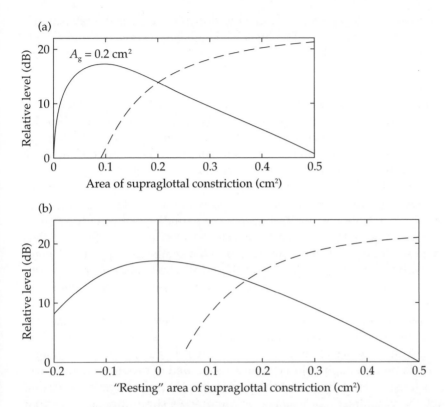

Figure 7.2 Relative amplitude as a function of the area of a turbulence-producing constriction in the vocal tract. The solid lines show the amplitude of turbulence produced at the constriction, the dashed lines the amplitude of glottal turbulence, each as a function of the size of the constriction. (a) shows results of a simulation which assumes that the vocal tract surfaces are inflexible; (b) shows similar results, assuming that the constriction area may be widened by air pressure behind the constriction. A_g is the area of the glottis. After Stevens, 1989, p. 22.

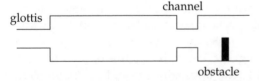

Figure 7.3 A tube model of an obstacle fricative, showing a channel which produces a jet of air and an obstacle in the path of the jet. This model is most often associated with the sibilants [s] and [ʃ].

Shadle (1991) makes a distinction between fricatives that involve a "wall" source, in which a jet of air hits a wall in the vocal tract – the velar fricative [x] is an example – and "obstacle" sources for sounds that involve making a jet of air that hits the front teeth. To this we might add "lip" source fricatives like [v] and [f], in which the airstream is directed against the upper lip. These different types of fricatives all involve an obstacle. The only nonobstacle fricatives are produced at the lips and perhaps at the glottis. Note how difficult it is to make bilabial and glottal fricative noises loudly. In fact, in some languages – Navajo is an example – the phoneme /h/ is produced with oral fricative allophones [x] or [ç]. I have also seen this in careful speech in American English.

The differences between "wall" and "obstacle" fricatives have to do with the orientation of the obstacle relative to the direction of airflow. For instance, in a "wall" fricative the obstacle is nearly parallel to the airflow, while in an "obstacle" fricative the obstacle is more nearly at right angles to the airflow. Catford (1977) notes that a sharp angle between the orientation of the obstacle and the stream of air produces vortices in the airflow which, because they are periodic, give rise to a complex periodic wave having a definite pitch (as in an organ pipe). He argues that spectra of [s] produced by people with and without their false teeth (p. 155) are evidence that airflow past the teeth produces periodic vortices in the airflow which contribute high-frequency components to the spectrum of [s]. Shadle (1991) manipulated the location of the obstacle, and found quite large spectral changes associated with the filtering properties of the front cavity, both in front of and behind the aperiodic noise source. So Catford's proposal, although interesting, has not been confirmed.

Voiced fricatives are relatively unusual in the languages of the world, undergo a variety of phonetically motivated alternations, and are surprisingly difficult to produce. The difficulty, which may underlie the cross-linguistic and phonological patterns, arises because high volume velocity is needed to produce the turbulent noise characteristic of fricatives, and the vibrating vocal cords impede the flow of air through the vocal tract. For instance, if you drape a sheet of paper over your face, you can easily blow it off with a voiceless labio-dental fricative [f], but not with a voiced labio-dental fricative [v]. This is because during voicing the vocal cords are shut (or nearly so) as much as they are open. Therefore, given a comparable amount of air pressure produced by the lungs (the subglottal pressure), the volume velocity during voicing is much lower than it is when the glottis is held open. Because a certain degree of airflow is necessary in order to produce turbulence, voiced fricatives may lose their frication, and become glides. Note that this alternation does not necessarily involve a change in the degree of vocal tract constriction; you can produce either a voiceless fricative or a voiced glide with the same degree of vocal tract narrowing. McDonough (1993) proposed that this underlies alternations between voiced lateral approximants and voiceless lateral fricatives, the phonological distinction in some languages being one of voicing, which, due to the width of the lateral channel, leads to frication in the voiceless case and nonfrication in the voiced case.

7.2   Place of articulation in fricatives

When you make a series of fricatives starting from a pharyngeal constriction and moving the constriction forward to the alveolar ridge, you may be able to hear a change in the "pitch" of the fricative. (The analysis in this section follows that of

Heinz and Stevens, 1961.) The frequency change that you hear in a series like this is caused by changes in the filtering action of the vocal tract, and in particular, changes in the length of the front cavity of the vocal tract. In the tube model shown in figure 7.3, the front cavity extends from the narrow channel, the point of constriction, to the lips, and includes the obstacle.

Because the sound source is located in the front cavity, and because the acoustic coupling between front and back cavities is weak when the vocal tract is tightly constricted, the acoustic filtering action of the vocal tract in fricatives is determined primarily by the resonant frequencies of the front cavity (which you can calculate using the same formula as we used in chapter 5 to calculate vowel resonances, $F_n = (2n - 1)c/4L$). When the fricative constriction is located in the pharynx, the front cavity is long, and consequently has lower resonant frequencies than when the fricative constriction is located further forward in the mouth.

Acoustic coupling

Constrictions can cause acoustic impedance in much the same way that they can cause aerodynamic impedance, but these two types of impedance are different. For example, when you keep your mouth and nose closed and produce a short voiced sound, as during a voiced bilabial stop or a grunt, no air escapes from your vocal tract, but sound does. This is because the sound waves produced at the glottis can vibrate through your cheeks, like your neighbor's stereo does through your walls. (Note the acoustic filtering effects of solid objects; only low-frequency noise gets through.) Acoustic coupling refers to acoustic impedance: the degree to which sound is transmitted across some acoustic barrier. In fricatives, the front and back cavities are not very well coupled, and the acoustic impedance at the vocal tract constriction is relatively large. So although air flows through the constriction, relatively little sound is transmitted to or from the back cavity. Consequently, the resonant frequencies of the back cavity have relatively little impact on fricative spectra.

Figure 7.4 shows fricative spectra produced in a two-tube model. The number beside each of the spectra indicates the length (in cm) of the front cavity. The shorter the front cavity, the higher the frequency of the lowest spectral peak (except for the case with no front cavity, labeled 0, which is discussed below). Also note that the amplitude of the spectral peak is highest when the front cavity length is 2.2 cm. Stevens (1989) attributes the lower amplitude when the front cavity is 1.5 cm long to increased acoustic damping in the radiation of high-frequency sounds from the lips (relative amplitude in the spectrum increases 6 dB per octave as sound radiates from the lips). He says that the decreased amplitude of fricatives with constrictions further back in the mouth is due to "a smaller degree of coupling of the source to the front-cavity resonance" (p. 24). I don't know why this would happen. When I first saw this figure, I incorrectly assumed

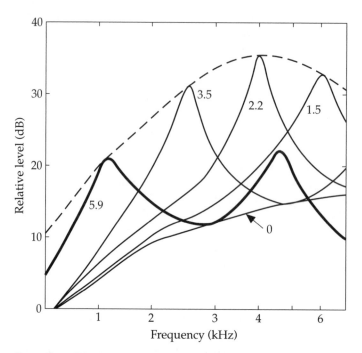

Figure 7.4 Fricative spectra produced by a tube model similar to the one shown in figure 7.3. The spectra were produced with five models having different front cavity lengths, which are indicated (in cm) for each of the spectra. After Stevens, 1989, p. 25.

that he had modeled the acoustic damping that occurs when the walls of the acoustic tube are soft. Then you would expect tubes with more wall space (tubes with longer front cavities) to have greater acoustic damping, hence resonances with wider bandwidths, and therefore lower peak amplitudes (more about bandwidth in chapter 9).

Even though the location of acoustic energy in the spectrum tells us most of what we need to know about the place of articulation of the fricative, the presence or absence of vocal tract resonance peaks can also be an acoustic cue for place of articulation. Some fricatives produced very far forward in the mouth, like [f], may have no vocal tract filtering at all (see the spectrum of a fricative with a front cavity length of 0 in the figure above). Unlike vowels, the location of the noise source in fricatives varies. In the pharyngeal fricatives [ħ] and [ʕ] the source of acoustic energy is in the pharynx, and the resonating vocal tract is relatively long; while in labial fricatives like [f] and [v], which are made with turbulence at the lips, there is almost no vocal tract in front of the constriction to filter the sound. Hence the spectra of labial fricatives do not have peaks, but rather have energy spread over a large frequency range (like the spectrum of turbulence shown in figure 7.1). Jakobson et al. (1952) termed spectra with a single prominent resonance peak [compact] and those with little or no vocal tract filtering or conversely a long front cavity and thus several spectral peaks [diffuse].

Figure 7.5   X-ray tracings of [s] and [ʃ] in English, showing the sublingual cavity in [ʃ]. Adapted from Straka, 1965, p. 38.

Lip rounding has the same acoustic effect in fricative production that it does in vowel production; it lowers formant frequencies. So, for instance, the [s] of American English *see* is unrounded, while in *sue* it has coarticulatory rounding from the following [u]. Perhaps you can hear the difference between these two [s] sounds. Interestingly, the other strident fricative (in which the upper teeth serve as an obstacle) in American English, [ʃ], is usually produced with lip rounding in addition to having a different place of articulation. This additional articulation *enhances* the acoustic difference between [s] and [ʃ].

The production of [ʃ] in many languages is also affected by the presence of a sublingual cavity (see figure 7.5). In an informal survey of native English speakers around the Ohio State University Linguistics Lab I found that seven out of eight speakers produce [ʃ] with a sublingual cavity. (You can check this in your own pronunciation by the toothpick test. During the pronunciation of a sustained fricative, insert a toothpick between your teeth, and poke your tongue. If you poke the bottom of the tongue, you have evidence that there is a sublingual cavity in the production.) This space below the tongue effectively adds length to the front cavity of the vocal tract, and thus lowers its resonance frequency. So, even though [s] and [ʃ] have quite similar places of articulation, their acoustics are markedly different, because [ʃ] has a sublingual cavity and [s] has either a very small sublingual cavity (for tongue-tip up [s]) or none at all (for tongue-tip down [s]).

7.3   Quantal theory and fricatives

Two nomograms relating articulatory parameters of fricative production to fricative acoustics show quantal regions (regions of acoustic stability). The first, relating degree of constriction to the relative amplitude of the fricative, was reproduced as figure 7.2 above. This figure illustrates the quantal basis for distinctions in "manner of articulation" or "stricture." Over a range of constriction sizes, any degree of constriction results in essentially the same amplitude of frication noise,

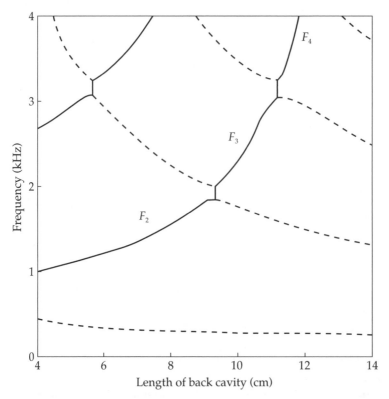

Figure 7.6 The effects of acoustic coupling of the front and back vocal tract cavities on the resonance properties of fricatives. The resonant frequencies of the front cavity are shown by the solid lines, and the resonant frequencies of the back cavity are shown by the dashed lines. The lowest dashed line is the Helmholtz resonance of the back cavity. From Stevens, 1989, p. 26.

especially when the effects of intra-oral air pressure on channel size are taken into consideration (see figure 7.2b, where the stable region extends from -0.1 cm^2 to 0.1 cm^2). This finding suggests that frication is one of only a few natural acoustic outputs of the vocal tract; the others are silence in noncontinuant sounds and laminal airflow in sonorant sounds. In other words, the different degrees of stricture to which we refer in phonetic and phonological theory are natural acoustic classes, because different ranges of constriction sizes result in stable types of acoustic output. (Note that the glottal "fricatives" [h] and [ɦ] are fricatives if we define the class as sounds produced with turbulent airflow; but, unlike other fricatives, they are nonconsonantal in the sense that they have coupled front and back tubes (i.e. vowel-like spacing between formants), while consonantal sounds have no front/back coupling and thus wider spacing between formants, with sudden changes in the number of formants at the boundaries between consonantal and nonconsonantal segments.)

The second nomogram is shown in figure 7.6. This figure shows the effects of coupling between the front and back tubes in a two-tube model of fricatives. As mentioned earlier, as the length of the front cavity decreases, the frequency of the peak resonance in the fricative increases. Although back cavity resonances do not appear in the radiated fricative sound, or appear only weakly, the coupling between the front and back cavities does have an effect on the nomogram. Note the discontinuities in the front cavity resonance frequencies that occur when the resonant frequencies of the front and back cavities converge.

When a constriction is located in the back part of the vocal tract (i.e. when the front cavity is long and the back cavity is short, as shown in the left part of the nomogram), the lowest resonant frequency of the fricative will match the second formant of nearby vowels. So, in [xa] (where [x] is a voiceless velar fricative) the lowest resonance peak in the fricative matches the frequency of F_2 at the onset of the following vowel. In constrictions further forward in the vocal tract, the formant affiliation of the fricative's resonant peak changes when the front cavity resonance intersects with back cavity resonance. Consequently, the peak resonance frequency in [ç] (a voiceless palatal fricative) matches the frequency of F_3, rather than F_2 of the following vowel. Because the resonant frequencies of two coupled tubes are never exactly the same, there is a jump in the nomogram at each intersection of front and back cavity resonances (at each change in formant affiliation of the fricative's peak resonance). According to Stevens (1989), such discontinuities mark the boundaries between places of articulation that have a relatively stable articulation-to-acoustic mapping for fricatives.

7.4   Fricative auditory spectra

Figure 7.7 shows acoustic (LPC) spectra of six voiceless fricatives found in Egyptian Arabic. These spectra were taken from recordings of a female speaker reading these words:

[fæ:t]	*to pass*
[sæ:b]	*he left*
[ʃæ:b]	*to get gray, grow old*
[χæ:l]	*maternal uncle*
[ħæ:l]	*situation*
[hæ:t]	*give me*

Several aspects of fricative acoustics which have been discussed in this chapter are apparent in these spectra. Notice that the spectrum of [f] is unlike the other spectra, in that it does not have any one region of spectral prominence. Energy tends to be distributed throughout the spectrum. The other spectra vary in terms of the frequency location of the peak of spectral energy, with [s] showing the highest frequency concentration and [h] showing more low-frequency emphasis than the others. This follows the prediction that we made earlier, based on the assumption that the resonant frequencies of the front cavity determine the vocal tract filter function in fricatives, and consequently that as the place of articulation in fricatives moves from front to back, the peak of spectral energy in fricatives

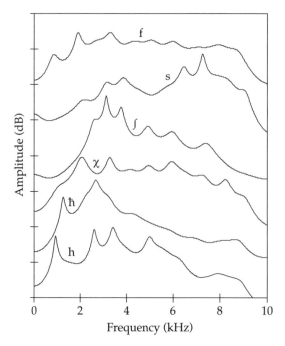

Amplitude (dB)

Frequency (kHz)

Figure 7.7 Acoustic spectra of Egyptian Arabic fricatives from the words listed in the text. The spectra were produced by LPC analysis from waveform windows in the middle of the fricative noises, and have been offset on the amplitude scale (disregarding overall amplitude differences) to allow for greater ease in comparing the spectral shapes. The interval between ticks on the vertical scale is 20 dB.

will go from higher to lower frequency. Note also that the spectrum of [h] is like a vowel spectrum although with greater relative amplitude in the higher formants than we usually see in vowels.

Note in figure 7.7 that the fricatives [s] and [ʃ] differ substantially. The spectral peak in [ʃ] occurs at about 3.5 kHz, while the spectral peak in [s] is near 8 kHz, although there is also a minor peak at about 4 kHz. Many researchers have noted that it is difficult to measure the acoustic characteristics of fricatives (particularly coronal fricatives), because there may be several spectral peaks as in this production of [s], and from utterance to utterance one or the other of these may have greatest amplitude. It has also been noted that there may be a substantial range of inter-speaker variability in the frequencies of the spectral peaks in fricatives. These observations have led to the development of center-of-gravity techniques for the characterization of fricative spectra (Forrest et al., 1988; Jassem, 1979). In this connection it is interesting to consider the auditory representation of fricatives. As discussed in chapter 3, two of the main characteristics of the human auditory system are the nonlinearity of the auditory frequency scale and the widths of the auditory critical bands for high frequencies. These two characteristics combine to radically alter the auditory representation of fricatives as compared with their acoustic representation.

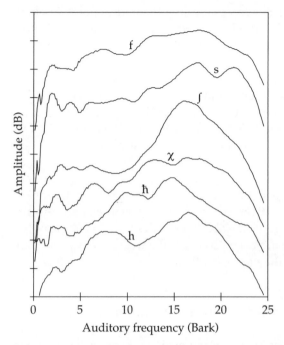

Figure 7.8 Auditory spectra of the fricatives illustrated in figure 7.7. The auditory spectra were taken from the same waveform windows used to calculate the LPC spectra in figure 7.7, and, like the spectra shown there, have been offset on the amplitude scale to facilitate comparisons of spectral shape. The interval between ticks on the vertical scale is 20 dB.

Figure 7.8 shows auditory spectra of the same fricative segments that were shown in figure 7.7. These spectra were calculated using the same waveform windows that were used in producing the LPC spectra shown earlier, and demonstrate many of the same characteristics that we saw in figure 7.7. For instance, [f] has a flatter, more diffuse spectrum than do the other sounds, and the remaining fricatives show spectral prominences of progressively lower frequency as the constriction moves from front to back. However, unlike the acoustic spectra of these sounds, the auditory spectra seem to be more evenly spaced. Note also that the difference between the two broad regions of spectral energy in [s] is reduced. It seems reasonable to suggest that some of the difficulties associated with the acoustic characterization of fricatives are reduced, if not eliminated, by the auditory transformation. In this connection, it is worth noting that the spectral analysis technique most often used in commercially available speech recognition systems employs a form of auditory analysis called Mel frequency cepstral coding (Davis and Mermelstein, 1980), because the Mel scale, which is an auditory frequency scale, reduces confusion at the higher frequencies where speakers' productions may differ significantly, with minimal effect on the listener's percept.

In addition to practical issues having to do with measuring fricative noises and recognizing them in computer speech recognition programs, the auditory representations shown in figure 7.8 raise an interesting theoretical point. Looking at the acoustic spectra in figure 7.7 (and realizing that the range of fricative distinctions found in Arabic is representative of the range found in the languages of the world), it seems odd that more of the frequency range above 5 kHz is not used to distinguish fricative noises. Why are the spectral peaks of four of the fricatives crowded together below 4 kHz, while only the spectral peak of [s] is above this? Only half of the frequency range below 10 kHz seems to be used to signal distinctions among fricatives. This is especially odd in view of the fact (mentioned earlier) that [ʃ] is usually pronounced with a sublingual cavity and lip rounding, which serve to lengthen the front cavity of the vocal tract, thus lowering the frequency of the spectral prominence associated with this sound. This oddity of the acoustic spectra is not true of the auditory spectra in figure 7.8. There the spectral peaks of the fricatives are more nearly evenly spaced in the available frequency range. This suggests that fricatives with spectral peaks between those of [s] and [ʃ] are uncommon in the languages of the world not because they are hard to produce, but because they are hard to hear.

7.5   Dimensions of fricative perception

The placement of the English voiceless fricatives in perceptual space is illustrated in figure 7.9. This figure shows the results of two multidimensional scaling analyses – one for American English listeners (black letters on white background) and one for Japanese listeners (white letters on dark background). All of the listeners heard the same American English stimuli, and identified them as "f," "th," "s,"

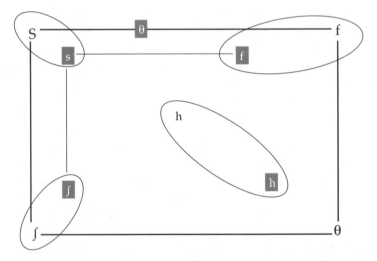

Figure 7.9   Multidimensional scaling analysis of data reported by Lambacher et al. (2001). The space for American English listeners is plotted with black letters on white background, and the space for Japanese listeners is plotted with white letters on a dark background. The stimuli were produced by an American English speaker.

"sh," or "h." I made this figure from the confusion matrices published by Lambacher, et al. (2001) using the method described in chapter 4.

Look first at the perceptual space for American English listeners. These listeners had very few confusions among these sounds (about 94 percent correct identifications) so in this two-dimensional space we have the five fricatives spread out about as much as they could be – one in each corner and one in the middle. Notice that the sibilant, or strident, fricatives are together on the left and the non-sibilant oral fricatives [f] and [θ] are together on the right (for the American English listeners). The two fricatives with relatively more front constrictions [s] and [f] are at the top of the space and the two backer fricatives [ʃ] and [θ] are at the bottom.

The likely acoustic correlates of the horizontal dimension is frication noise amplitude – [s] and [ʃ] have louder frication noise than do the others. The vertical dimension may be related to the spectral shape of the frication noise – [ʃ] and [θ] having more low frequency components. [h] has a very diffuse spectrum which might explain how it comes to be in the middle of the space.

Now consider the results for the Japanese listeners (white letters). First notice that the Japanese space fits inside the American English space. This means that overall the Japanese listeners were less able to correctly identify these American English sounds. Next notice that three of the fricatives are positioned at the corners of the space as they were for English listeners. These are [f], [s], and [ʃ]. For these sounds the Japanese and American English spaces have about the same shape.

Now look at [θ]. In the Japanese space [θ] is closer to [s] than to any other fricative, while for American English listeners no two fricatives were more widely separated than these. A couple of things are going on. First, [θ] is not a surface allophone in Japanese. Unlike any of the other fricatives in this study it is a totally foreign sound. Second, though the [s] and [θ] frication noises are quite different from each other, their formant transitions (an important cue for place of articulation) are quite similar. The Japanese listeners may be relying on this similarity and ignoring the frication noise differences that seem so significant for the American English listeners.

What we see in this brief example is that fricatives are organized perceptually on dimensions that are at once phonetic and linguistic. The linguistic dimensions do not run counter to the acoustic/auditory dimensions of the fricatives, but we see how a linguistic system of contrasts may lead listeners to rely on certain auditory properties and neglect others.

Exercises

Sufficient jargon

Define the following terms: turbulent airflow, turbulent noise, turbulence, particle velocity, volume velocity, laminal flow, channel turbulence, obstacle turbulence, aerodynamic impedance, wall source fricatives, acoustic coupling, [compact], [diffuse], sublingual cavity.

Short-answer questions

1   In the sagittal sections in figure 7.5, indicate the points of highest particle velocity (assum-
    ing a constant volume velocity through the mouth). Show the point of noise generation in
    these vocal tract configurations, assuming that the diameter of the opening is proportional
    to the width shown in the figure.
2   The analysis of fricative acoustics presented here assumed that the front and back cavities
    were not acoustically coupled, because fricative constrictions are narrow. At what points in
    time during the production of a fricative is this assumption most likely to be wrong? And
    how would you expect the acoustic coupling of the front and back cavities to affect the
    fricative spectrum?
3   Discuss voiced fricatives and [h] in light of the suggestion given in this chapter that stricture
    classes like stop, fricative, etc. are best defined acoustically.
4   Compare figures 7.6 and 6.4. In chapter 6, I suggested that the regions of stability for
    vowels occur at the points of convergence of the lowest front and back resonances; but in
    this chapter these points were defined as the least stable regions in the mapping from
    articulation to acoustics for fricatives. For instance, a vowel with a back cavity of 7 cm is
    considered to be in an unstable region of the nomogram, but a fricative with that length of
    back cavity is considered to be in a stable region. How does this observation relate to
    attempts to find features of place of articulation which are equally applicable to vowels and
    consonants?

CHAPTER 8

Stops and Affricates

Stops and affricates have more complicated articulatory and acoustic properties than vowels or fricatives. The preceding chapters on vowels and fricatives disregarded dynamic aspects of the sounds, and treated them as static events, because it is fairly reasonable to think about vowels and fricatives in terms of static acoustic targets, or articulatory postures. This is not so with stops and affricates. The main articulatory posture during a stop is complete closure of the vocal tract, the acoustic consequence of which is silence (or, if the vocal folds are vibrating, muffled voicing). However, languages use a greater variety of stops than this simple description predicts, utilizing different places of articulation, mechanisms for producing stop release sounds, and accompanying noises. For this reason it is useful to identify three stages in the articulation of stops and affricates, which correspond to three intervals of time (see figure 8.1), each of which can be characterized in terms of the acoustic theory of speech production as a combination

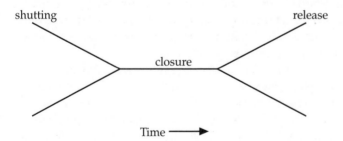

Figure 8.1 Three stages in the time course of stop or affricate production. The lines indicate articulators moving toward each other during the shutting stage and separating during the release stage.

of a sound source and a vocal tract filtering function. The first stage is the movement of an articulator toward a stop closure (the **shutting** movement); the second
is the **closure** itself; and the third is the **release** of the closure.

8.1   Source functions for stops and affricates

8.1.1   Phonation types

Before discussing source functions for stops and affricates, we will look at the
acoustics of different phonation types, even though phonation type can be varied
distinctively in vowels and fricatives as well as stops. Three main types of voicing
occur cross-linguistically. They are modal, creaky, and breathy voicing. Modal
voicing occurs in all languages, and some distinguish it from one or both of the
other types of voicing. Although vocal cord vibration is an immensely complex
phenomenon (for instance, see Bless and Abbs, 1983, and Laver, 1980), I will focus
on just one aspect which seems to be most relevant acoustically – the amount of
time that the vocal folds are open during each glottal cycle. In passing it should
be noted that Ladefoged and Maddieson (1996) choose a related measure – peak
oral airflow – as the most reliable way to measure different phonation types.
As you may recall from the discussion of aerodynamics in fricatives, oral volume
velocity is related to glottal impedance; voiceless sounds have greater oral
airflow than voiced sounds. So glottal impedance in voiced sounds varies, depending on the amount of time that the vocal folds are open during each glottal cycle
(assuming comparable subglottal air pressure).

In modal phonation the vocal folds are closed during half of each glottal cycle
and open during the other half (approximately). Thus, the proportion of time
that the glottis is open (the open quotient) during each cycle is 0.5. In creaky
voicing the vocal folds are held together loosely, like two pieces of calf liver, and
air bubbles up through them. This results in a longer closed phase of the glottal
period and a comparably shorter open phase (and thus a smaller open quotient).
In breathy voicing the vocal folds vibrate, but without much contact (for some
people the vocal folds do not completely close during breathy voicing), and thus
the glottis is open for a relatively long portion of each glottal cycle. Figure 8.2
shows synthetic glottal waveforms (produced by a speech synthesizer) that illustrate the differences between small, medium, and large open quotients. These
waveforms all have a fundamental frequency of 100 Hz.

We know from Fourier's theorem that any change in the shape of the voicing
waveform (which is a complex periodic wave) results in a spectral change as
well. This is illustrated in the spectra of these synthetic voicing waveforms shown
in figure 8.3. (Note that if we keep the pulse shape the same and change the pitch
period by stretching or shrinking the closed phase, only the spacing between the
harmonics will change; the shape of the spectrum will stay the same.) The breathy
voicing waveform shown in figure 8.2 is more like a sine wave than either creaky
or modal voicing. This is reflected in the spectrum shown in figure 8.3 by the

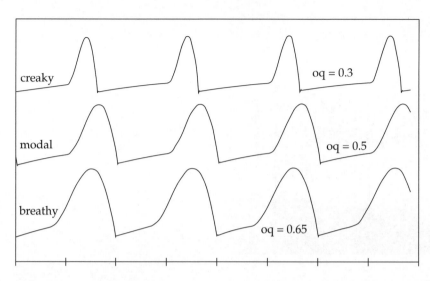

Figure 8.2 Glottal waveforms produced by varying the open quotient (oq) of the glottis in a speech synthesizer. In the top waveform, creaky voice is simulated by keeping the glottis closed over 70 percent of each glottal cycle, with a quick glottal opening occurring in the remaining 30 percent of the cycle. In the second and third waveforms the open quotient is increased to 50 percent and 65 percent of the glottal cycle, respectively, simulating modal and breathy voice.

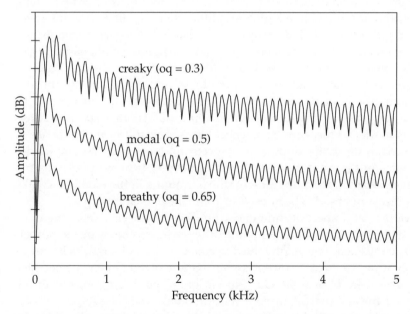

Figure 8.3 Power spectra of the synthetic glottal waveforms shown in figure 8.2. These spectra are offset on the amplitude axis to make them easier to distinguish. The interval between ticks on the vertical axis is 10 dB.

Figure 8.4 A spectrogram of the English word "what" showing creaky voice.

dominance of the first harmonic. All the other harmonics have lower amplitude. This is because the first harmonic in a complex wave is a sine wave that has the same frequency as the fundamental frequency of the voicing waveform (in this case, 100 Hz); and since the breathy voice waveform is somewhat sinusoidal, the first harmonic tends to dominate the spectrum. The creaky voice waveform is least like a sine wave, and this is reflected in its spectrum, where the second, third, and fourth harmonics have higher amplitude than the first. The difference between the amplitude of the first harmonic and that of the second harmonic is a reliable way to measure the relative breathiness or creakiness of phonation, especially for low vowels, where the first formant doesn't influence the amplitude of either harmonic very much. Changes in F_0, loudness, and vowel quality can alter the relative amplitudes of the first and second harmonics, so you have to be careful when you use this measure of phonation type. Another spectral difference, which is harder to measure in practical terms (because of the influence of vocal tract resonance), is the slope of the spectrum. Note that the amplitudes of the harmonics in the breathy voiced spectrum drop off more quickly as frequency increases than do the amplitudes of the harmonics in the modal or creaky spectra. This measure has also been used to compare phonation types.

These waveform and spectral differences produced by a change in the open quotient are typically accompanied by some differences in other acoustic properties as well. The muscular tension involved in creaky voice often results in slower vocal fold vibration, so creaky voice may have a lower fundamental frequency than modal or breathy phonation. On a spectrogram the voicing pulses during creaky voice are further apart than they are in modal voicing (see figure 8.4 for an illustration of this). This difference is a reliable acoustic correlate of creaky voice in English. Similarly, the long open period in breathy voice results in a bit of time in each glottal cycle during which the glottis is open enough to allow a high rate of airflow, and thus some glottal frication (aspiration noise) is produced during each glottal cycle in breathy voicing (hence the name).

Stops and affricates may differ distinctively in different languages, depending on the phonation type with which they are produced. These voicing distinctions can occur in any of the three stages of stop and affricate production.

8.1.2 Sound sources in stops and affricates

The most common source of acoustic energy during the **shutting** stage of stop consonant production is voicing. This may be modal voicing or, less frequently, creaky or breathy voicing. Pre-glottalized stops are produced with creaky voicing in the closing stage, and pre-aspirated stops have a bit of aspiration noise (turbulence generated at the glottis) during the closing stage.

During **closure**, voicing is the only possible sound source. Otherwise the closure is voiceless. The reasons for this limitation are both aerodynamic and acoustic. The presence of audible aspiration is unlikely, because there is no direct acoustic coupling between the noise source and the air outside the mouth. So the walls of the vocal tract muffle any turbulence that might be generated during closure. The aerodynamics of stop closure also prevents aspiration or other frication noise sources from occurring. Since the vocal tract is completely blocked during stop closure, air flowing from the lungs has nowhere to go. This is especially problematic for the production of aspiration, which takes a lot of airflow; but it also prevents any other fricative noise from being produced. Voicing is also aerodynamically impeded, though not prevented, during stop closure. Air flows through the vocal folds and into the occluded vocal tract, but soon the vocal tract fills up, so the air from the lungs has nowhere to go, and voicing can no longer be maintained. Thus, in spectrograms, we often see some voicing early in a stop closure, which fades away by the end of the closure. Voicing either persists through only part of the closure, or the speaker performs a maneuver to expand the oral cavity, and thus extend the period of voicing. Implosives (glottalic ingressive sounds) result from one oral cavity-expanding maneuver: larynx lowering (Lindau, 1984). Other available oral cavity expansion maneuvers include (a) tongue-root advancement and (b) reduction of tension in cheek or pharynx muscle (to allow for passive expansion during the closure). Pre-nasalized stops such as [mb] or [ᵐb] sometimes arise historically from voiced stops in which voicing during the closure is facilitated by opening the nose (note that the oral stop gesture extends through both the nasal and the stop in [mb]). So this variant realization of the closure stage may also be motivated by the aerodynamic constraints on voicing during stop closure.

During the **release** portion of stops, several different types of sound source are found. The first of these, stop release burst, is not optional, and is unique to stop releases. The stop burst is produced when increased air pressure in the vocal tract is released. Air rushes out of the mouth at high speed, producing a pressure impulse that lasts only 2 or 3 milliseconds. Thus the burst noise marks the moment of stop consonant release. Like the shutting stage, release can also be voiced (with modal, creaky, or breathy voicing) or aspirated.

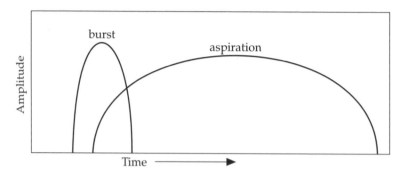

Figure 8.5 Schematic illustration of the burst and aspiration noises in the release of an aspirated stop.

It is important to distinguish the two sound sources in aspirated stops. Burst noise is produced at the consonant place of articulation (like fricative noise), whereas aspiration noise is produced at the glottis. Thus the vocal tract filter for the two types of sound sources is different. Also, the burst is very short in duration, whereas aspiration noise may be quite long. For a few milliseconds after a stop closure is released, the constriction is too narrow to allow the amount of airflow needed to produce aspiration at the glottis. Thus, immediately after the release, conditions are right for the burst (high-pressure buildup, very narrow opening) but not for the aspiration; while later, as the constriction is opened further, conditions are right for aspiration (when the constriction is open enough for a high volume of airflow). The relative dominance of these two sound sources during the release phase of aspirated stops is illustrated in figure 8.5.

Sounds produced with the mouth closed

This raises the question of how it is that we can hear, and see on spectrograms, voicing during stop closures. The voicing that we hear during stop closures is like the music you hear when your upstairs neighbor plays the stereo too loud. Just as with stop voicing, there may be no direct air passage for the sound (unless both the upstairs and downstairs windows are open); but you can hear the stereo because the floor (you ceiling) transmits the music at the floor's resonant frequencies. However, this wall-rattling music does not sound the same as it would if you were in the room with the loudspeakers. All you can hear is the boom, boom, boom of the bass. You hear the beat, but not the melody. This is because floors and walls have low resonant frequencies (they are big massive things), so they resonate best to low notes. Similarly, when the vocal cords vibrate during a stop closure, the walls of the vocal tract transmit the sound, but only the low-frequency components. Thus, in spectrograms, voicing during stop closures appears as a low-frequency band, called a "voice bar," at the bottom of the spectrogram.

There are several ways to make stop release bursts. The best-understood type of release burst is found in pulmonic stops, such as we have in English. In ejectives (glottalic egressive sounds) the air pressure behind the stop closure, which is generated by closing the glottis and raising the larynx during the stop closure, is usually greater than that in pulmonic stops, and the resulting burst has greater amplitude. This is especially true of dorsal ejectives, because higher intra-oral (in the mouth) air pressures can be produced during dorsal ejectives than during ejectives with other places of articulation, because the mouth cavity is smaller in [k] than in [p]. So perhaps it isn't surprising that dorsal ejectives are more common than other ejectives in the languages of the world. (John Ohala objects to this explanation of the prevalence of ejective [k'] in the languages of the world, suggesting that release bursts of back stops are generally more salient perceptually than those of front stops, because the vocal tract in front of the constriction is longer, hence the burst contains more information about the articulation.) Ejectives are also characterized by two release bursts: the oral release and the glottal release (Lindau, 1984; McDonough and Ladefoged, 1993). So sometimes these "glottalized" stops are transcribed with a glottal stop following the oral stop symbol, [kʔ], which in the IPA is [k'].

The stop release bursts of implosives (glottalic ingressive sounds), on the other hand, are weaker than those of pulmonic stops. This is so, presumably, because the intra-oral air pressure buildup during the closure state is usually not very large in implosives. It is important to realize that the weak burst does not necessarily indicate ingressive airflow, but only the tendency for implosives to involve not much change in intra-oral air pressure during stop closure.

Click release bursts are typically much louder than any other type of release burst, because the difference between air pressure in the mouth and atmospheric air pressure is quite large in clicks. Since clicks are produced with a very small air cavity between the tongue and the roof of the mouth, a relatively small movement of the tongue produces a very large change in intra-oral air pressure, and hence makes it possible to produce a loud ingressive release burst.

8.2   Vocal tract filter functions in stops

Two types of vocal tract filtering affect the acoustic properties of stop consonants. First, the vocal tract configuration immediately following closure shapes the spectral qualities of the release burst. Second, the vocal tract configurations and movements just before and after stop closure shape formant movements in the shutting and release stages of stop production.

The burst is essentially a transient which has a flat spectrum (see chapter 1). This noise source is then shaped by the resonances of the portion of the vocal tract in front of the stop closure, because the closure at the time of the release is still quite narrow, and thus the front and back cavities of the vocal tract are not acoustically coupled (figure 8.6). Thus, bursts are acoustically similar to fricatives. Labial stops do not have a front cavity, so the spectrum is determined by

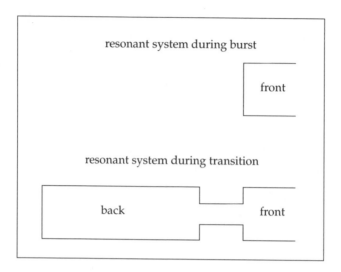

resonant system during burst

front

resonant system during transition

back   front

Figure 8.6   Acoustic tube models of the burst and the release stages in stops.

the acoustics of the sound source, with no vocal tract shaping. Therefore, the release bursts of labial stops have no formant peaks, and energy is spread diffusely at all frequencies. Dental and alveolar stops have a short front cavity, hence high-frequency peaks of spectral energy. Palatal and velar stops have a longer front cavity, thus lower-frequency peaks in the spectrum and generally more formant structure than other stop bursts.

In the portion of the stop release after the burst and in the shutting stage, the front and back cavities of the vocal tract are acoustically coupled, and the sound source is located at the glottis, both for voicing and for aspiration. Therefore the acoustic properties of these stages in stop consonants are better understood in terms of the models we used to discuss vowel formant values (perturbation theory and two-tube models). As their names imply, shutting and release are movements, not postures; so, like diphthongs, the information they contain about place of articulation is seen in formant movements, rather than particular formant values. And of course the characteristics of a movement depend on its beginning and ending points. This is illustrated in figure 8.7.

Delattre et al. (1955) used these formant patterns to control the output of a speech synthesizer. The patterns illustrate the formant movements and steady states needed to produce the syllables listed in the figure. Recall from chapter 6 that the second formant (vocal tract resonance) is high in the front vowels, and the first formant is high in the low vowels. The point that this figure makes is that the formant movements (transitions) that contribute to the perception of a particular stop place of articulation depend on the identity of the following vowel. This is especially striking in the case of [d]. When the F_2 of the vowel is high, the F_2 transition rises into the vowel; but when the F_2 of the vowel is low, the transition falls. Delattre et al. found that the perceptually important part of the transition is not actually present in the acoustic signal, but can be derived from a set of

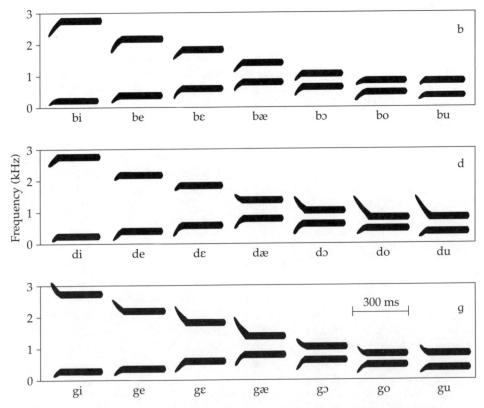

Figure 8.7 F_1 and F_2 transition patterns in stop release used to synthesize [b], [d], and [g] followed by various vowels. Adapted from Delattre et al., 1955, p. 770, and published with permission.

syllables such as those shown in figure 8.7. For example, if you superimpose the F_2 trajectories of syllables, starting with [d], and extend the F_2 trajectories back in time, they seem to intersect at about 1,800 Hz. They called this hypothetical starting frequency the F_2 locus frequency. In their study the F_2 locus frequency for labials was 720 Hz, while velars had a higher F_2 locus at 3,000 Hz. Their estimate for velars is wrong, because they were using synthetic stimuli that had only two formants; but the pattern is right. Labials have a low-frequency locus, alveolars a middle-level locus, and velars a somewhat higher one.

The fact that the locus is not actually reached is due to changes in the acoustic coupling of the front and back cavities during stop production. As mentioned earlier, the vocal tract's acoustic properties change suddenly when the front and back cavities are coupled. At the instant of stop release, the front and back cavities are uncoupled, so the resonant frequencies of the back cavity do not have an impact on the speech spectrum; but as the closure is opened further, the front and back cavities become coupled. This explains the fact that the release burst of [d] has higher-frequency resonances than does the release burst of [g], while [g] has a higher F_2 locus than [d]. The release burst of [d] is shaped by a front cavity resonance (which has a high frequency), but the F_2 locus is associated with a back cavity resonance. Both the burst and the F_2 locus of [g] are associated with a front cavity resonance.

The rapid change in the coupling of front and back cavities also explains why all stop consonants have a low-frequency F_1 near the stop closure interval. During closure the two cavities are uncoupled, thus there is no first formant (because the first formant is a Helmholtz resonance – see chapter 6). The Helmholtz resonator that gives us F_1 starts with a very narrow neck (and thus a low F_1). As the constriction widens, the neck of the Helmholtz resonator increases, and thus the frequency of F_1 increases. Also, as the closure is released and the constriction becomes wider, the front and back cavities become acoustically coupled. The opposite happens during the shutting stage. The first formant starts relatively high, and falls as the constriction is formed.

Formant transitions

All formants are lower near the stop closure in **labial** (bilabial) stops. In terms of perturbation theory, you can think of this as a result of having a constriction located at a velocity node (at the lips) for all the vocal tract resonances. The F_2 locus for **coronal** (dental and alveolar) stops is a bit higher than the second resonant frequency of a uniform tube. The F_3 near the closure in coronal stops is also higher than in the uniform tube. These effects are predicted in a two-tube model with a constriction near the front of the vocal tract (figure 6.4). In **dorsal** (palatal and velar) stops there is a convergence of F_2 and F_3 near the stop closure, because the location of the closure is near the intersection of the front and back cavity resonances. Of course, the formant loci for variants of American English velars (before front and back vowels) vary.

8.3   Affricates

The release phase of a stop may have frication rather than voicing or aspiration. This is the only difference between stops and affricates. The frication noise in affricates is usually produced at the same place of articulation as the stop (with some room for variation as the affricates [ts] and [tʃ] show). This cannot be a defining property of affricates, however, because heterorganic affricates do occur. For example, McDonough and Ladefoged (1993) found that the stops transcribed [tˣ] in Navajo are acoustically and phonologically affricates. Heterorganic fricatives are also found in Northern Sotho and related languages. The main acoustic distinction between an affricate and a sequence of a stop and a fricative is that the amplitude of frication noise rises quickly to full amplitude in affricates, and more slowly in fricatives. This property has been called **rise time**, and is illustrated in figure 8.8.

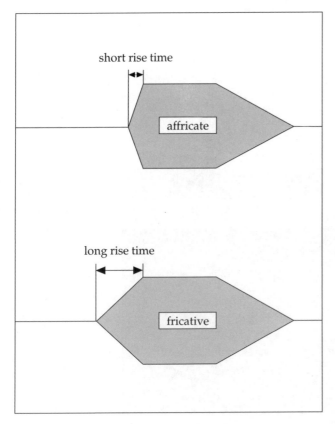

Figure 8.8 Schematic illustration of the difference between affricate and fricative waveform envelopes. Amplitude rises quickly in affricates, more slowly in fricatives.

8.4   Auditory properties of stops

Figure 8.9 shows spectrograms and cochleagrams of three nonsense syllables [ba], [da], [ga] spoken by a native speaker of English. The figure illustrates a couple of important differences between auditory and acoustic representations of stops. First, as we saw in chapter 6, in auditory representations the F_2 region is relatively more prominent than it is in spectrograms (even though both display frequencies from 0 to 11 kHz). In figure 8.9 this is apparent in the large F_2 movements in the cochleagram after the stop releases. So although F_2 transitions may appear to be fairly indistinct in spectrograms (especially when a large frequency range is displayed), they are enhanced in the auditory representation. We might note that our calculation of the F_2 locus discussed above was based on acoustic formant trajectories. Presumably, because the auditory frequency scale is nonlinear, auditory F_2 locus frequencies will be different from these acoustic estimates. I don't know of any detailed investigation of this possibility, but it is a

Figure 8.9 Spectrograms (top) and cochleagrams (bottom) of [ba], [da], [ga] produced by a male speaker of English, illustrating some differences between acoustic and auditory representations of stop consonants.

consideration which may have an impact on our understanding of the notion "locus frequency."

Second, release bursts are more prominent in the cochleagrams than they are in the spectrograms. This is a result of the automatic gain control mechanism of the peripheral auditory system – adaptation. After a brief period of silence, the auditory system responds more strongly than it does in a period of continuing sound. So onsets in general produce a large response in the auditory system. In stops this enhances the importance of release bursts; but notice also that even vowel initial syllables may produce "release bursts" in the auditory system. This may explain why synthetic, "burstless" syllables sound like they begin with a stop consonant; the auditory system supplies a burst, even though it is missing in the acoustic signal.

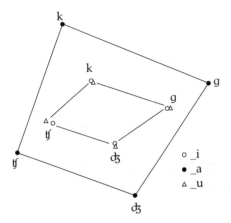

Figure 8.10 Perceptual maps of [k], [g], [ʧ], and [ʤ] in different vowel contexts. These maps were made from the confusion matrices published by Guion (1998).

8.5 Stop perception in different vowel contexts

The velar stop [k] often changes to the palatal affricate [ʧ] when the following vowel is [i]. This change, written as:

$$k \rightarrow ʧ \, /\_i$$

is called **palatalization** and has occurred in many languages. Guion (1998) cites palatalization changes in Slavic, Indo-Iranian, Salish, Bantu, English, Mayan, and Chinese.

On careful consideration it seems obvious that palatalization has an articulatory motivation. The [k] becomes fronted because the next sound is the front vowel [i]. This explanation is strengthened by the observation that other front vowels like [e] and [æ] also condition this change in many languages. However, it is a little odd that the result of palatalization [ʧ] has a place of articulation that is further forward than the conditioning environment [i]. If palatalization was a purely articulatory process by which [k] becomes more like [i], then we would expect the end result to be a palatal stop [c]. What's up with that?

What's up with that is that perception plays a role in palatalization. One of the best demonstrations of this comes from Guion's (1998) confusion matrices. Figure 8.10 shows the results of separate MDS analyses for confusions among [k], [g], [ʧ] and [ʤ] as produced by a group of American English speakers and perceived by a group of American English listeners. The CV syllables were presented in noise (with a +2 dB signal to noise ratio), and listeners identified the syllable initial consonant as "k," "g," "ch" or "j."

The perceptual space in figure 8.10 is organized so that the velar stops are at the top and the palato-alveolar affricates are at the bottom. The horizontal dimension has the voiceless consonants on the left and the voiced consonants on the right. These consonants were much easier for listeners to identify when the following vowel was [ɑ]. That's why the square connecting the solid dots (the _ɑ environment) is so much larger than the space formed by connecting the dots for the _i and _u environments. The perceptual space shrinks when the vowel following the stops was [i] or [u].

Now what does this result say about palatalization? I think what it means is that the reduced perceptual distance between [k] and [tʃ] in the [_i] environment means that listeners may be less likely to notice when a speaker produces [tʃ] instead of [k] in this environment. The articulatory motivation still holds – [i] exerts fronting pressure. But we also have a perceptual "licensing" effect, so that the [k] to [tʃ] change is permitted in [i] environment because this change is not likely to be very noticeable.

Exercises

Sufficient jargon

Define the following terms: three stages of stop production, modal voice, creaky voice, breathy voice, open quotient, phonation types, aspiration noise, pre-glottalized stops, pre-aspirated stops, prenasalized stops, implosives, voice bar, stop release burst, ejectives, glottalized stops, clicks, intra-oral, formant transitions, locus frequency, rise time.

Short-answer questions

1 Measure the spectral tilts of each of the spectra in figure 8.3. Fit a straight line as well as possible to the harmonic peaks in each spectrum, then measure the tilt as amplitude change per 1,000 Hz.

2 Find the F_2 locus frequency of [d] from the stylized spectrograms shown in figure 8.7. To do this, collapse the figure from right to left like an accordion or a radio antenna, so that all the syllables are superimposed over [di]. I used my ruler to mark two points for each syllable, the F_2 at the beginning of the transition and the F_2 at the end of the transition, with approximately the same horizontal spacing that they had in the original. Connecting these two points per syllable reproduces the formant transitions for each CV syllable. To find the locus frequency, extend the lines back in time. They should intersect (near the frequency axis labels), and the intersection point is the F_2 locus of these examples of [d].

3 If a disproportionate number of languages had [k] but not [p] (Arabic is an example), how would that relate to Ohala's view on the rarity of velar ejectives?

4 Do affricates have stop release bursts? How might short rise time lead to decreased auditory salience of release bursts in affricates?

5 Many languages allow more stop contrasts in syllable onsets (before the vowel) than in syllable codas. This is called "onset licensing." Which would you predict to be more restricted in coda position: place contrasts (bilabial versus dental, etc.) or laryngeal contrasts (aspirated versus unaspirated)? A relevant observation is that onset stops are always released, whereas coda consonants may or may not be released.

CHAPTER 9

Nasals and Laterals

In chapter 8 we saw that stops and affricates are more complicated than vowels and fricatives, because their productions have more than one stage and more than one type of sound source. Nasals and laterals are also more complicated than vowels or fricatives, but in a different way: it is their vocal tract filtering characteristics that are more complicated. As in the last chapter, we will start with a (relevant) digression.

9.1   Bandwidth

One way in which the vocal tract filtering function in nasals is different from that in oral vowels is that the width of the resonance peak (the bandwidth) of the first formant is larger in nasals. So, before discussing the acoustic properties of nasals, we will discuss formant bandwidths.

Figure 9.1 shows an undamped sine wave and two damped sine waves. Amplitude in the damped sine waves decreases over time. Like pushing a child on a swing: you give the swing a push, and before long it stops swinging, because the energy you put into the push is dissipated by a natural resistance to the swinging motion – the friction as the swing (and child) moves through the atmosphere. The damped sine wave labeled "heavy damping" loses amplitude more quickly than the one labeled "light damping." To follow our analogy, the more heavily damped wave corresponds to swinging on the earth, the lightly damped wave to swinging on the moon (where the atmosphere is less dense, and therefore the effect of friction is smaller).

Recall that the spectrum of a sine wave has a line showing the amplitude and frequency of the wave. As you might guess, given the fact that a damped sine

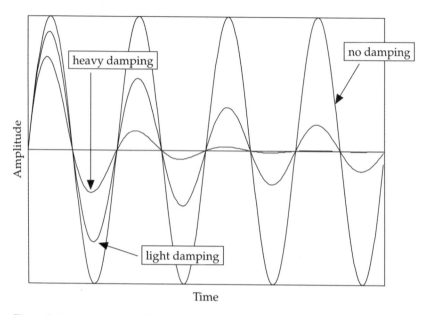

Figure 9.1   An undamped sine wave compared with two damped sine waves identical in frequency and phase.

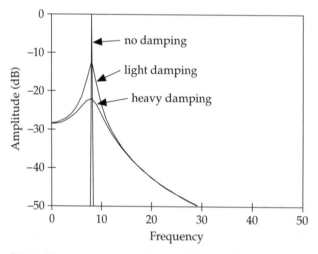

Figure 9.2   Power spectra of the waveforms shown in figure 9.1. Note that increased damping corresponds to wider bandwidth of the spectral peak.

wave does not have an exactly sinusoidal form, damped sine waves have more complex spectra than undamped sine waves. Figure 9.2 shows that the spectra of damped sine waves have peaks at the same frequencies as the undamped sine wave, but also have energy spread over other frequencies near the frequency of the peak. The spectral result of damping the sine wave is to broaden the peak around the sine wave's frequency. With an undamped sine wave the peak is infinitely narrow, but with more and more damping the peak gets wider and wider. Look again at the waveforms in figure 9.1. The one that corresponds to swinging on the moon (light damping) looks more like a pure sine wave than the other. Because the "light damping" waveform is more similar to a sine wave than the "heavy damping" waveform, the "light damping" spectrum looks more like a sine wave spectrum. That is, it has a narrower peak. The wave that decays more rapidly looks less like a sine wave in both the waveform display and the spectrum.

Because the walls of the vocal tract are soft, they absorb some of the sound energy produced by the vibrating glottis. (The inertia of air, in and out of the vocal tract, also absorbs some of the sound energy.) The sound pressure waves that resonate in the vocal tract might go on vibrating infinitely, but the sound energy is absorbed by the soft walls and the inertia of air, the way friction absorbs the energy in the push of the swing. Thus, when we look at vocal tract resonances (formants), they have certain bandwidths, because the resonant frequencies of the vocal tract are damped. If the walls of the vocal tract were hard (and hence could reflect sound energy without absorbing it), the formants would have much smaller bandwidths.

The formant bandwidths during nasal sounds are wider than those in nonnasal sounds, because the vocal tract with the nose open has greater surface area and greater volume. The greater surface area of the vocal tract means that the walls of the vocal tract absorb more sound than in nonnasal sounds, and the greater volume of air means that the inertia of air within the vocal tract absorbs more sound as well. However, as we will see, the apparent widening of the F_1 bandwidth in nasalized vowels is more complicated than this.

9.2   Nasal stops

We will start with the uvular nasal [ɴ], because this is the simplest nasal consonant to describe. (The analysis I'm presenting here follows loosely the more technical description given in Fujimura, 1962. Note that Lindqvist-Gauffin and Sundberg, 1976, suggested that the sinus cavities play an important role in nasal acoustics, a factor which is discussed in passing in the analysis presented here.) When the uvula is lowered and the dorsum of the tongue raised to produce an uvular nasal, the vocal tract can be described, to a first approximation, as a uniform tube that is closed at the glottis and open at the nostrils. If we know the length of the tube, we can calculate its resonant frequencies, because this is a quarter-wave resonator (like the vocal tract configuration for schwa, in chapter 5). In X-ray pictures published by Fant (1960) the distance from the uvula to the nares is 12.5 cm, and the distance from the uvula to the glottis is 9 cm, giving a total length from glottis to nares of 21.5 cm. Thus the four lowest resonant frequencies of the tube (where c is the speed of sound in air in cm/sec) are:

$F_1 = c/4l = 35,000/4 \times 21.5 = 35,000/86 = 407$ Hz
$F_2 = 3c/4l = 1,221$ Hz
$F_3 = 5c/4l = 2,035$ Hz
$F_4 = 7c/4l = 2,849$ Hz

These estimates of the formants of [N] are inaccurate in some respects, because our assumption that the vocal tract can be modeled by a uniform tube is wrong. We can improve the estimates by assuming that there is a constriction of the nasal tract at the nostrils (the nose has permanent "lip rounding"). By perturbation theory, since we know that there is a velocity maximum at the nostrils for each of the resonances, we expect that each of the resonant frequencies will be lower than the calculations above suggest. This is only one way in which the anatomy of the nasal passage differs from a uniform tube. It is hard to make quantitative predictions about the formant frequencies of [N], because the shape of the nasal passage varies from person to person – and for any one person, from day to day, when you have a cold – but we can identify one basic property. The formant values will be spaced more closely in the uvular nasal than they are in schwa; for a male vocal tract the interval between formants in schwa is about 1,000 Hz, whereas the interval between formants in [N] is about 800 Hz. Figure 9.3a shows the spectrum of [ŋ] in the Thai word [ŋa] "ivory." This spectrum, as predicted, has four approximately evenly spaced formants below 3 kHz, and their frequencies are about the same as the frequencies we calculated for a uniform tube that is 21.5 cm long.

The low amplitude of F_3 and the even lower amplitude of the eighth harmonic may be due to the frontal sinus cavities (more on this later). Figure 9.3b shows a spectrogram of the syllable that the spectra in figure 9.3a were taken from. In the spectrogram you can see that the nasal stop [ŋ] has lower frequency F_1 and F_2 than does the vowel [a]. There is also an apparent gap in the nasal spectrum at about 1.5 kHz, corresponding to the weakened F_3 in the spectra, and the formants above 3 kHz are too weak to appear in the spectrogram. Nasal consonants are generally weaker (i.e. have lower amplitude) than vowels. This is partly due to the fact that the larger resonant passageway causes increased damping of the formants, but the main reasons why nasal consonants are weaker than vowels are (1) the fact that in nasals the vocal tract has side cavities like the sinuses, and (2) the vocal tract is more constricted in nasal consonants than in vowels (the constriction is at the opening to the nasal passages).

The main difference between [N] and [m] is that the mouth cavity forms a side branch in the resonant tube. The X-ray tracing in figure 9.4a shows the mouth cavity, and the tube model in figure 9.4b shows the mouth as a side branch to the tube formed by the pharynx and the nose. The mouth cavity can be modeled as a tube closed at one end (the lips) and open at the other (the uvula), with a length of about 8 cm. We can therefore calculate the resonances of the mouth cavity as we did for schwa (in chapter 5) or for [N] (in the preceding paragraphs). Assuming that the mouth cavity is an 8 cm long uniform tube

(a)

(b)

Figure 9.3 (a) FFT and LPC spectra of the nasal murmur in [ŋ] produced by a female speaker of Thai. Note that there are four formants below 3 kHz. (b) A spectrogram of the utterance from which these spectra were taken. The spectra were taken from the midpoint of the nasal murmur, which is labeled "ŋ."

(a)   (b)

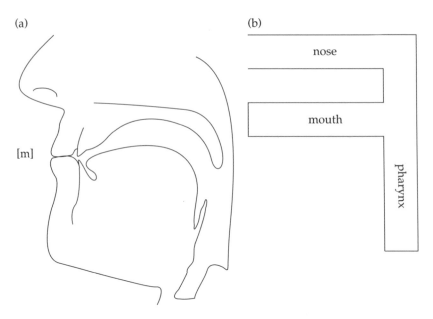

Figure 9.4   (a) An X-ray tracing of the positions of the articulators during [m] (adapted from Straka, 1965, p. 34). (b) A tube model of this vocal tract configuration.

that is closed at one end and open at the other, its lowest resonant frequency is $c/4l = 35,000/(4 \times 8) = 1,094$ Hz, and the second resonant frequency is $3c/4l = 3,281$ Hz.

The resonant frequencies of the mouth cavity in nasals are not like resonant frequencies that we've seen before, because the mouth cavity is a side branch of a larger resonant tube. It doesn't open directly to the atmosphere. So frequency components in the sound source that are near the resonant frequencies of a side cavity resonate in the side branch without making an appearance in the acoustic output of the acoustic tube system. They are "absorbed" in the side branch. So the frequency components in [m] that are near the resonant frequencies of the mouth are canceled, and become anti-resonances (also called "anti-formants") in the acoustic output. Formants show up in the spectrum as peaks of sound energy, and anti-formants show up as pronounced spectral valleys. It is important to make a distinction between active anti-resonance and passive lack of resonance. There are valleys in the spectrum of schwa, but these are the result of a lack of resonance; some frequency components are simply not enhanced as much as others. In contrast to this, there are some frequency components in [m] that are actively subtracted from the spectrum.

Another effect of an anti-formant in the spectrum is that the amplitudes of all the formants above it are reduced (Fant, 1960, estimated that the amplitudes of all formants higher than the anti-formant are reduced by about 1.6 dB per octave), because they are riding on the "skirt" of the anti-formant. Osamu Fujimura (personal communication) reminded me that this amplitude reduction is not a general property of anti-formants, but depends on the frequency separation of the resonance and anti-resonance which are contributed by a side cavity. The account of anti-formants given here glosses over some details about how anti-formants arise from side cavities (having to do with acoustic coupling and the fact that anti-resonances are always paired with resonances), and so the 1.6 dB per octave reduction is taken without proof as a good general estimate of the spectral effect of an anti-formant. Thus, nasal sounds have more energy at the low end of the spectrum. The increased bandwidths that we see in nasal sounds also cause the formant amplitudes to be reduced. In spectrograms, then, nasal sounds appear lighter than the nearby oral vowels.

Anti-formants and anti-matter

When I bring up anti-formants in a class, someone always asks me if this is like anti-matter. The answer is, "I don't know, maybe." If, as on the starship *Enterprise*, matter and anti-matter cancel each other out, then it might be reasonable to say that anti-formants are a bit like anti-matter. Lord Rayleigh (1896) attributed the sound-canceling aspect of anti-formants to "interference of direct and reflected waves" (p. 211). The direct waves in the case of nasal stops are the sound waves traveling through the pharynx-nose tube, and the reflected waves are the waves which are resonating in the mouth cavity. Because of the polarity shift at the open end of a tube closed at one end (recall the bull whip example), the reflection of the resonances of the mouth cavity has exactly the opposite phase of the same frequency component in the pharynx-nose tube. So when one wave is positive, the other is negative, and when you add them together, they cancel each other out. In this way, I suppose, anti-formants are like anti-matter (whatever that is).

The frequencies of some anti-formants in the spectrum of a nasal stop depend, therefore, on the length of the mouth cavity. For instance, the mouth cavity in [n] is about 5.5 cm long. A uniform tube that is closed at one end and open at the other and that has a length of 5.5 cm has resonant frequencies at 1,591 Hz and 4,773 Hz; thus we expect the spectrum of [n] to have an anti-formant at about 1,600 Hz and another at about 4,800 Hz. As mentioned above, the mouth cavity in [m] is about 8 cm long, so we would expect to see an anti-formant in the spectrum of [m] at about 1,100 Hz and another at about 3,300 Hz. In this way the frequencies of the anti-formants are cues to the place of articulation in these nasals.

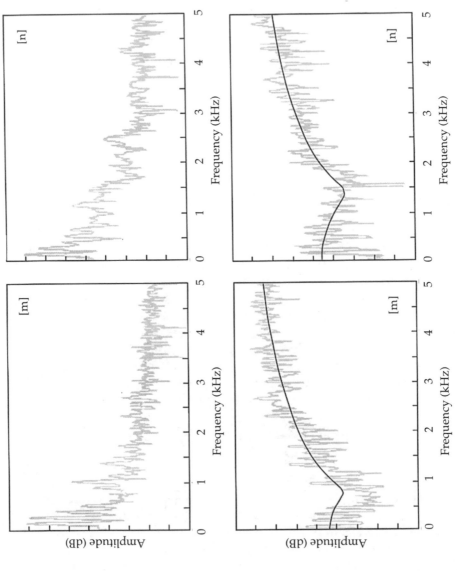

Figure 9.5 Anti-formants in [m] and [n] in English. The left panels are of [m], the right panels of [n]. The top panels show FFT spectra of the nasals, the bottom panels the spectrum of the LPC inverse-filtered spectra and the estimated filtering effect of the anti-formants. The interval between ticks on the vertical scale is 10 dB. Adapted from Qi, 1989, figs 24–7, and published with permission.

Figure 9.5 shows results from one method of determining the frequency of the anti-formants in nasals (Marple, 1987; Qi, 1989). In this method, called auto-regressive/moving average analysis, an LPC analysis is performed to find peaks in the nasal spectrum; then the signal is filtered to remove the formants, and LPC analysis is used to find anti-formants. The figure shows spectra of [m] and [n] produced by a male speaker of English in the top two panels. In the bottom panels we see spectra of the signals after removing the formants, using a tech-nique called "inverse filtering," together with LPC spectra showing the lowest anti-formants in each consonant spectrum. This figure shows that the measured frequencies of the first anti-formants in [m] and [n] are a little lower than pre-dicted. In [m] the first anti-formant (A_1) is at about 750 Hz, whereas we predicted that it would be at about 1,100 Hz; and in [n] A_1 is at about 1,400 Hz, whereas the predicted value was 1,600 Hz. So the simple tube model that we have been using is a little off; but the general pattern predicted by the model is borne out – A_1 is lower in [m] than it is in [n].

Given this discussion of how anti-formants are caused by side cavities in the vocal tract, the importance of the nasal sinuses should be apparent. The sinuses function like Helmholtz resonators, so their resonant frequencies – the frequen-cies of the anti-formants that they contribute to the spectrum – depend on the volume of the sinus and the dimensions of its opening. It turns out that there is quite a bit of individual variation in the sizes of the sinuses and of the openings into them. So it is difficult to give any firm estimates of the frequencies of the anti-formants contributed by the sinuses. Lindqvist-Gauffin and Sundberg (1976) found that for one speaker the maxillary sinus contributed an anti-formant at about 500 Hz, and the frontal sinus contributed an anti-formant at about 1,400 Hz.

Figures 9.6 and 9.7 show FFT and LPC spectra and spectrograms of [m] and [n] produced by a female speaker of Thai in the words [maː] *come* and [naː] *rice field*. In these spectra the presence of anti-formants is indicated by arrows. Note that anti-formants produce a mismatch between the LPC spectrum and the Fourier spectrum, because LPC analysis assumes that the vocal tract filter function has no anti-formants. Earlier we noted that the mouth cavity in [m] should in theory have resonances at about 1,100 Hz and 3,300 Hz, which will appear in the spec-trum of [m] as anti-formants, while the spectrum of [n] should have anti-formants at higher frequencies (1,600 Hz and 4,800 Hz). These predictions are generally borne cut in the spectra shown in figure 9.6. Note that an anti-formant may or may not appear as a white band in the spectrogram. If there are no formants near the anti-formant, it appears white in the spectrogram (figure 9.7b); but if the frequency of the anti-formant is about the same as the frequency of a formant, the net result is to weaken the formant peak.

As with [ɴ], this analysis of [m] and [n] is inaccurate in some respects, because of the simplifying assumptions of the tube model. Still, the main properties of nasals are captured in this analysis – low F_1 (sometimes called the "nasal formant"), close spacing between formants, and the presence of anti-formants – whose frequencies are determined by the place of articulation of the stop.

Figure 9.6 (a) FFT and LPC spectra of the nasal murmur in [m] produced by a female speaker of Thai. The estimated frequencies of the anti-formants are indicated by arrows. (b) A spectrogram of the utterance from which these spectra were taken. The spectra were taken from the midpoint of the nasal murmur, which is labeled "m."

Figure 9.7 (a) FFT and LPC spectra of the nasal murmur in [n] produced by a female speaker of Thai. The estimated frequency of the lowest anti-formant is indicated by an arrow. (b) A spectrogram of the utterance from which these spectra were taken. The spectra were taken from the midpoint of the nasal murmur, which is labeled "n."

Perceiving anti-formants

Repp (1986) found that listeners could identify nasal murmurs extracted from syllables starting with [n] and [m] correctly 72 percent of the time. When the vowel formant transitions (see chapter 8) were included, performance was more than 95 percent correct, and even with only 10 ms of the vowel following the nasal murmur performance was 94 percent correct. These results suggest that the frequencies of the anti-formants in [m] and [n] are important perceptual cues for these consonants. Or maybe not. Seventy-two percent correct in a task where guessing would give you 50 percent correct means that the nasal murmur may not have been very informative in most of the nasals – only 12.5 percent of the sounds have to have some identifiable cue for place of articulation to get this result.

One reason why nasal murmurs may not be very good indicators of place of articulation is that in normal experience (as opposed to most laboratory speech-perception experiments) communication takes place amid background noise. So anti-formants (or, more properly, the spectral shape changes caused by anti-formants) may not be very audible in the signal, because background noise fills in the anti-formant valleys. It may also be that listeners do not pay much attention to the detailed spectral shape in nasal stop murmurs, because the spectrum includes some idiosyncratic information about the (current) size and shape of the speaker's sinuses which is pretty irrelevant as a cue for stop place of articulation in that it is not very predictable across speakers.

9.3   Laterals

We can analyze the acoustics of laterals in a way that is very similar to the analysis of nasals presented in the last section, because lateral sounds are produced with a side branch that introduces an anti-formant in the output spectrum. Figure 9.8a shows an X-ray tracing of [l]. In his analysis of the acoustics of laterals, Fant (1960) assumed that a small pocket of air on top of the tongue acts as a side branch to the main acoustic channel which curves around one or both sides of the tongue. Ultrasound images of the tongue shape during laterals (Stone, 1991) shows a side-to-side rocking motion of the tongue during [l] in American English, which suggests that the opening around one side is more open than the other. I have seen palatograms of laterals in Tamil and Taiwanese which indicate that both sides of the tongue are lowered to some extent, but that there may be some asymmetry in the sizes of lateral openings on the left and right sides of the tongue. Nonetheless, a pocket of air remains on top of the tongue, and this serves as an anti-formant-producing side branch, just as the mouth cavity does in nasal consonants.

This configuration of the vocal tract can be modeled with a uniform tube that has a short side branch, where the side branch is the pocket of air on top of the

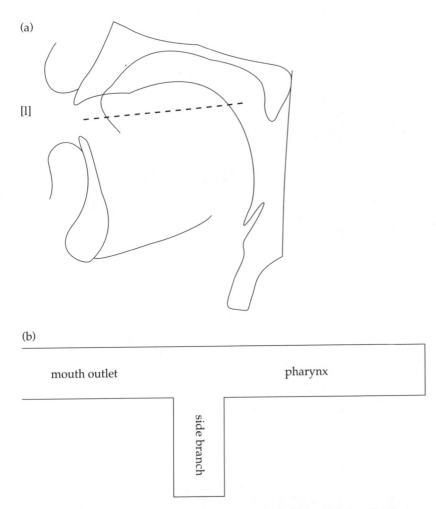

(a)

[l]

(b)

mouth outlet   pharynx

side branch

Figure 9.8 (a) An X-ray tracing of [l] in Icelandic. The dotted line suggests that there is a lateral opening around at least one side of the tongue. Adapted from Petursson, 1973, p. 91.
(b) A simplified tube model of this vocal tract configuration. A side channel is formed by a pocket of air over the tongue, while the outlet channel is formed around one or both sides of the tongue.

tongue. The tube model is shown in figure 9.8b. Fant (1960) estimated that the length of the pocket was 4 cm and the length of the vocal tract 16 cm (10 cm from the glottis to the branch and a lateral outlet cavity of 6 cm) for one speaker. Thus the resonances of the vocal tract (assuming, counterfactually, a uniform tube) are 531, 1,594, and 2,656 Hz. You may recognize these as resonant frequencies of schwa. The pocket, modeled as a tube open at one end and closed at the other, resonates at 2,125 Hz (c/4l, where c = 35,000 cm/sec and l = 4 cm). Since this is a side cavity, this resonance becomes an anti-resonance in the output at the lips.

(a)

(b)

Figure 9.9   (a) FFT and LPC spectra of the lateral approximant [l] produced by a female speaker of Thai. The estimated frequency of the lowest anti-formant is indicated by an arrow. (b) A spectrogram of the utterance from which these spectra were taken. The spectra were taken from the midpoint of the lateral, which is labeled "l."

This tube model for laterals is somewhat oversimplified, because the outlet cavity has a smaller diameter than does the tube from the glottis to the lateral constriction. The most important acoustic consequence of this is that the frequency of the first formant is lower than it would be in a uniform tube. Syllable-final [l], in American English at least, is also produced with a dorsal constriction that lowers the frequency of the second formant. Still, the tube model's basic prediction is that the spectral "signature" of laterality will be an anti-formant between F_2 and F_3.

Figure 9.9 shows FFT and LPC spectra of [l] produced by the same speaker of Thai who produced the sounds shown in figures 9.3 and 9.6. These spectra were taken from the center of the lateral sound in [là:] "donkey". As indicated by the arrow, there is an anti-formant between F_2 and F_3. Note also that the formants are spaced relatively further apart in this figure than they were in the nasal sounds shown earlier; here we have only three formant peaks below 4 kHz, whereas in the nasal sounds there were four. There also seems to be an additional anti-formant in the spectrum at about 1 kHz, which may have resulted from asymmetry of the lateral openings around the tongue.

As with nasal sounds, the presence of an anti-formant causes the amplitudes of all higher formants to be reduced by about 1.6 dB. Also, the narrowness of the outlet cavity causes lateral sounds to be generally softer than vowel sounds. You can see these aspects of lateral acoustics in the spectrogram in figure 9.9b. One important difference between laterals and nasals is that the average spacing of the formants is wider in laterals than it is in nasals. This is because the primary resonant tube in nasals is longer than it is in laterals. In the examples we have been considering, the average spacing between formants in nasals is about 800 Hz, while in laterals it is 1,000 Hz.

9.4   Nasalization

We now turn to the most complicated configuration of the vocal tract found in speech (see also Fujimura, 1962; Maeda, 1993). In nasalized vowels there are two resonant systems operating at once, one composed of the pharynx cavity plus the mouth cavity, the other of the pharynx cavity plus the nasal cavity. This is illustrated in figure 9.10. In earlier discussions we have identified the resonant frequencies of these two systems. The pharynx plus mouth system – the oral tract – modeled as a uniform tube has resonances at about 500, 1,500, and 2,500 Hz; whereas the pharynx plus nose system – the nasal tract – modeled as a uniform tube has resonances at about 400, 1,200, and 2,000 Hz. All these formants are present in the spectrum of nasalized vowels. As we have already seen, the resonant frequencies of the oral tract can be modified by movements of the tongue and lips. Also, the resonances of the nasal tract can be modified by changes in the pharynx cavity, and we expect that the nasal tract resonances will be lower than the estimates that we derive from a uniform tube model because of the constriction of the nose at the nares. Still, the tube models predict that the spectrum of a nasalized vowel will have a lot of formants.

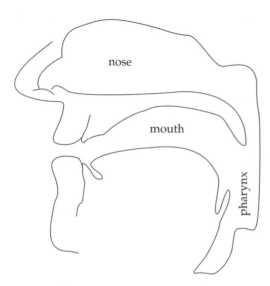

Figure 9.10 The vocal tract configuration in nasalized vowels. One acoustic system includes the pharynx and mouth; another simultaneous acoustic system includes the pharynx and nose.

As we saw above with nasal consonants, the closed mouth has resonances that become anti-resonances (anti-formants) in the spectrum of nasal consonants. In nasalized vowels the resonances of the nasal cavity become anti-formants, analogous to the anti-formants in nasal consonants except that now the mouth is more open than the nose, so the acoustic coupling between the mouth and the atmosphere is greater than is the coupling between the nasal passage and the atmosphere. The frequencies of the anti-formants in nasalized vowels are a function of the degree of coupling between the nasal cavity and the pharynx. With weak coupling the anti-formant frequencies are only slightly higher than the resonances of the nasal tract (400, 1,200, 2,000 Hz), but with stronger acoustic coupling – with the velopharyngeal port open wide – the frequencies of the nasal antiformants can be calculated assuming a tube that is open at one end (velopharyngeal port) and closed at the other (the nostrils). Because the distance from the uvula to the nostrils is about 12.5 cm, the two lowest resonant frequencies of the nose cavity are about $(c/4l =)$ 680 and $(3c/4l =)$ 2,040 Hz. To summarize, then, the predicted formant and anti-formant frequencies are shown in table 9.1.

Considering just the region below 1,000 Hz, where nonnasalized vowels have one resonance (the F_1), nasalized vowels have three spectral prominences: an oral formant (F_{1o}), a nasal formant (F_{1n}), and an anti-formant (A_1). The frequencies of these components depend on several factors. F_{1o} depends on the positions of the lips and tongue, and A_1 depends on the degree of nasalization. With a little bit of nasalization, the frequency of the A_1 is slightly higher than that of F_{1n}, and the frequency of A_1 increases as the degree of nasal coupling increases. The result of all this is that A_1 may cancel F_{1n} when there is slight nasalization and cancel F_{1o} at a higher degree of nasalization. So, for instance, an [a] with heavy nasalization

Table 9.1 Predicted frequencies of oral and nasal formants and nasal anti-formants in nasalized vowels (assuming uniform tubes and disregarding the effects of acoustic coupling).

	Nasal formants	Oral formants	Anti-formants
	(l = 21.5 cm)	(l = 17.5 cm)	(l = 12.5 cm)
F_1	407	500	680
F_2	1,221	1,500	2,040
F_3	2,035	2,500	-

can appear on a spectrogram to have a much lower F_1 than normal because F_{1n} is low (and will always be low, regardless of the vowel) and A_1 is high enough to cancel much of the energy of F_{1o}.

This type of complicated interplay between nasal formants, oral formants, and nasal anti-formants that occurs in the region of F_1 also happens at other frequencies. Perhaps it is no surprise that the number of distinctive nasal vowels in languages is usually smaller (and never larger) than the number of oral vowels. There is no articulatory problem in producing nasalized vowels, but they are acoustically and perceptually more complex than oral vowels.

One consequence of the interplay of formants and anti-formants in the F_1 region of nasalized vowels that you can see in spectrograms is that the effective bandwidth of F_1 is increased (this is because there are usually two formants in the region, rather than one). The vowels in figures 9.3b, 9.6b, and 9.7b sounded very nasalized to me, and if you compare these spectrograms with the one in figure 9.9b, you may notice that the F_1 of [la] is easier to identify than the F_1 in the nasalized vowels. These closely spaced formants are like the F_1 and F_2 of [u], which seem to merge into one wide formant in spectrograms. Also, as we have seen with laterals and nasal consonants, the amplitudes of the formants are decreased because of the presence of an anti-formant.

Finally, we can note some phonological patterns which may be due to the acoustic properties of vowel nasalization. There is a tendency for vowel distinctions to be lost or neutralized in nasal environments; for example, in some dialects of American English, *pen* and *pin* have merged. Wright (1986) reports that the effect of vowel nasalization is a general shrinking of the perceptual vowel space; nasalized high vowels are lower in the space than are their nonnasalized counterparts, and nasalized low vowels are higher in the space than are their nonnasalized counterparts. This observation leads to a speculation about the acoustic origin of vowel shift patterns. Vowels in several languages, including English, have undergone chain shifts, in which vowels rise by one step and the high vowels break into diphthongs. Nondistinctive vowel nasalization may play a role in initiating these chain shifts, because low vowels tend to have a certain amount of passive nasalization – the velum is pulled open by the palatoglossus muscle when the tongue is lowered (Moll, 1962; see also Lubker, 1968). This passive nasalization may lead to a perceptual re-evaluation of the quality of low vowels because, with the nasalization, they get an addition nasal tract formant and anti-formant. In this way a chain shift may get a start as a push chain, because of the acoustic and perceptual effects of vowel nasalization.

9.5 Nasal consonant perception

Figure 9.11 shows perceptual maps for three of the languages investigated by Harnsberger (2001). In this study the stimuli were geminate medial nasals in an [i_i] context produced by a speaker of Malayalam. Listeners heard the stimuli in triplets like this:

A	X	B
immi	iŋŋi	iɲɲi

They were asked to decide whether the middle stimulus X was more stimilar to the first A or the last B stimulus. In this example, listeners usually chose B because the palatal nasal [ɲ] sounds more similar to the velar [ŋ] than to the bilabial [m]. We can take the number of times that [ɲ] and [ŋ] are judged to be "more similar" to each other as a measure of their proximity to each other in perceptual space, and use these data to make perceptual maps.

The maps in figure 9.11 were made by Harnsberger (2001), I rotated them so that [ŋ] and [m] have the same value on the vertical axis. To my eye, this makes it easier to compare the perceptual spaces for the different languages. These displays (only three of the seven groups of listeners tested by Harnsberger!) are rich with information. We'll just notice in these results a few aspects of the perceptual space for nasals. Keep in mind that we are plotting the perceptual spaces of the *exact same stimuli* – the only difference from map to map is that the listeners speak different languages.

Some general aspects of the spaces for Malayalam, Marathi, and English are the same (and were the same for the other groups of listeners in Harnsberger's study). For example, the coronal nasals fall in the top half of the space and the labial and dorsal nasals are in the bottom half (with the palatal somewhat ambiguous on this dimension). The horizontal axis corresponds roughly to place of articulation. For all of the listeners regardless of native language, [ŋ] and [ɲ] are close to each other, as are [n] and [n̪].

There are however, some interesting language-specific patterns of nasal perception in these data. First of all, notice how the location of the retroflex [ɳ] is different in Marathi as compared with English and Malayalam. For English and Malayalam, [ɳ] is located between the dental and alveolar nasals [n] and [n̪] and the bilabial nasal [m]. For Marathi, [ɳ] is located further from [m] than are [n] and [n̪]. This is just pure speculation on my part, but it may be that English and Malayalam speakers are attending to the falling VC third formant transition of [iɳ] of the [iɳɳi] stimulus and finding similarity between that and the falling VC formant transitions of [im], while Marathi listeners are attending to the release

Figure 9.11   Perceptual maps of nasals for speakers of Malayalam, English and Marathi. Segments that are not in the nasal inventory of the language are printed on a grey background. The IPA symbols [m, n̪, n, ɳ, ɲ, ŋ] for nasals are respectively bilabial, dental, alveolar, retroflex, palatal, and velar. (Redrawn from Harnsberger, 2001).

transitions in the CV interval of the [iɳɳi] stimulus which would put it more like the alveolar and dental nasals.

The other most noticeable language-specific aspect of these figures is that [n] and [n̪] are merged in the perceptual space of Malayalam. The situation here seems to be similar to the 214/35 tone neutralization in Chinese that we saw in Chapter 4 (see also Diehm and Johnson, 1997). Asher and Kumari (1997) note that though [n] and [n̪] both exist in Malayalam, they are in nearly complementary distribution and "the functional load carried by the contrast is small" (p. 416). Evidently, the low functional load of [n] and [n̪] contrast in Malayalam led these two sounds to be more similar to each other for Malayalam listeners than they were for listeners whose language enforces a distinction between these acoustically similar sounds.

Exercises

Sufficient jargon

Define the following terms: damping, band width, side cavity or branch in the vocal tract, anti-resonance, anti-formant, resonance "skirt," sinus, velopharyngeal port, oral tract, nasal tract, passive nasalization.

Short-answer questions

1 Which has the steeper "skirt" in figure 9.2, the heavy damping waveform or the light damping waveform?
2 Estimate the resonances of the nasal tract if the pharynx cavity is 8 cm long and the nasal cavity is 12 cm long.
3 Estimate the frequency of A_1 in a palatal nasal stop.
4 Speculate on the acoustic properties of palatal and velar laterals in light of the discussion in this chapter on alveolar laterals. Do you expect these sounds to have anti-formants?
5 Explain how vowels that have greater than normal glottal opening (breathy voiced vowels or the portion of a vowel adjacent to a high airflow segment like a voiceless fricative) might be subject to "spontaneous nasalization"? An example of spontaneous nasalization: French *rosse* (with the plural suffix *-ed*) "horses" was borrowed into Middle Breton as *roncet.* A hint: Consider how the acoustic effect of a longer than normal open phase in glottal vibration might be similar to the effect of opening the nose.

References

Asher, R. E. and Kumari, T. C. (1997) *Malayalam*, London: Routledge.

Bladon, Anthony and Lindblom, Björn (1981) Modeling the judgment of vowel quality differences. *Journal of the Acoustical Society of America*, 69, 1414–22.

Bless, Diane M. and Abbs, J. H. (1983) *Vocal Fold Physiology: Contemporary research and clinical issues*, San Diego: College Hill Press.

Braida, L. D., Sekiyama, K., and Dix, A. K. (1998) Integration of audiovisually compatible and incompatible consonants in identification experiments. *Proceedings of AVSP98*, Terrigal (New South Wales, Australia).

Brödel, M. (1946) *Three Unpublished Drawings of the Anatomy of the Human Ear*, Philadelphia: Saunders.

Campbell, R. (1994) Audiovisual speech: Where, what, when, how? *Current Psychology of Cognition*, 13, 76–80.

Catford, J. C. (1977) *Fundamental Problems in Phonetics*, Bloomington: Indiana University Press.

Chen, Mathew Y. (1976) From Middle Chinese to Modern Peking. *Journal of Chinese Linguistics*, 4, 113–277.

Chiba, T. and Kajiyama, M. (1941) *The Vowel: Its nature and structure*, Tokyo: Kaiseikan.

Cooley, J. W., Lewis, P. A. W., and Welch, P. D. (1969) The fast Fourier transform and its applications. *IEEE Transactions on Education*, 12, 27–34.

Cooper, F. S., Liberman, A. M., and Borst, J. M. (1951) The interconversion of audible and visible patterns as a basis for research in the perception of speech. *Proceedings of the National Academy of Science*, 37, 318–25.

Davis, S. and Mermelstein, P. (1980) Comparison of parametric representations for monosyllabic word recognition in continuously spoken sentences. *IEEE Transactions on Acoustics, Speech, and Signal Processing*, ASSP 28, 357–66.

Delattre, Pierre C., Liberman, Alvin M., and Cooper, Fanklin S. (1955) Acoustic loci and transitional cues for consonants. *Journal of the Acoustical Society of America*, 27, 769–73.

Diehm, E. and Johnson, K. (1997) Near-merger in Russian palatalization. *OSU Working Papers in Linguistics*, 50, 11–18.

Fant, Gunnar (1960) *Acoustic Theory of Speech Production*, The Hague: Mouton.

Flanagan, James L. (1965) *Speech Analysis Synthesis and Perception*, Berlin: Springer-Verlag.

Forrest, Karen, Weismer, Gary, Milenkovic, Paul, and Dougall, Ronald N. (1988) Statistical analysis of word-initial voiceless obstruents: preliminary data. *Journal of the Acoustical Society of America*, 84, 115–23.

Fry, Dennis B. (1979) *The Physics of Speech*, Cambridge: Cambridge University Press.

Fujimura, Osamu (1962) Analysis of nasal consonants. *Journal of the Acoustical Society of America*, 32, 1865–75.

Fujimura, Osamu and Lindqvist, Jan (1971) Sweep-tone measurements of vocal-tract characteristics. *Journal of the Acoustical Society of America*, 49, 541–58.

Green, K. P., Kuhl, P. K., Meltzoff, A. N., and Stevens, E. B. (1991) Integrating speech information across talkers, gender, and sensory modality: Female faces and male voices in the McGurk effect. *Perception & Psychophysics*, 50, 524–36.

Guion, S. G. (1998) The role of perception in the sound change of velar palatalization. *Phonetica*, 55, 18–52.

Hagiwara, Robert (1995) Acoustic realizations of American /r/ as produced by women and me. *UCLA Working Papers in Phonetics*, 90, 1–187.

Halle, M. and Stevens, K. N. (1969) On the feature "Advanced Tongue Root." *Quarterly Progress Report*, 94, 209–15. Research Laboratory of Electronics, MIT.

Harnsberger, James D. (2001) The perception of Malayalam nasal consonants by Marathi, Punjabi, Tamil, Oriya, Bengali, and American English listeners: A multidimensional scaling analysis. *Journal of Phonetics*, 29, 303–27.

Heinz, John M. and Stevens, K. N. (1961) On the properties of voiceless fricative consonants. *Journal of the Acoustical Society of America*, 33, 589–96.

Huang, Tsan (2001) The interplay of perception and phonology in tone 3 sandhi in Chinese Putonghua. In E. Hume and K. Johnson (eds.), *Studies on the Interplay of Speech Perception and Phonology, Ohio State University Working Papers in Linguistics*, 55, 23–42.

Jakobson, Roman, Fant, Gunnar, and Halle, Morris (1952) *Preliminaries to Speech Analysis*, Cambridge, Mass.: MIT Press.

Jassem, W. (1979) Classification of fricative spectra using statistical discriminant functions. In B. Lindblom and S. Öhman (eds.), *Frontiers of Speech Communication Research*, New York: Academic Press.

Johnson, Keith (1989) Contrast and normalization in vowel perception. *Journal of Phonetics*, 18, 229–54.

Johnson, Keith (1992) Acoustic and auditory analysis of Xhosa clicks and pulmonics. *UCLA Working Papers in Phonetics*, 83, 33–47.

Johnson, Keith, Ladefoged, Peter, and Lindau, Mona (1993) Individual differences in vowel production. *Journal of the Acoustical Society of America*, 94, 701–14.

Johnson, K., Flemming, E., and Wright, R. (1993) The hyperspace effect: Phonetic targets are hyperarticulated. *Language*, 69, 505–28.

Joos, Martin (1948) Acoustic phonetics. *Language*, 23, suppl. 1.

Klatt, Dennis H. and Klatt, Laura (1990) Analysis, synthesis, and perception of voice quality variations among female and male talkers. *Journal of the Acoustical Society of America*, 87, 820–57.

Ladefoged, Peter (1996) *Elements of Acoustic Phonetics*, 2nd edn., Chicago: University of Chicago Press.

Ladefoged, Peter and Maddieson, Ian (1996) *The Sounds of the World's Languages*, Oxford: Blackwell.

Ladefoged, Peter, DeClerk, J., Lindau, M., and Papcun, G. (1972) An auditory-motor theory of speech production. *UCLA Working Papers in Phonetics*, 22, 48–75.

Lambacher, S., Martens, W., Nelson, B., and Berman, J. (2001) Identification of English voiceless fricatives by Japanese listeners: the influence of vowel context on sensitivity and response bias. *Acoustic Science & Technology*, 22, 334–43.

Laver, J. (1980) *The Phonetic Description of Voice Quality*, Cambridge: Cambridge University Press.

Liljencrants, J. and Lindblom, Björn (1972) Numerical simulation of vowel quality systems: the role of perceptual contrast. *Language*, 48, 839–62.

Lindau, Mona (1978) Vowel features. *Language*, 54, 541–63.

Lindau, Mona (1979) The feature "expanded." *Journal of Phonetics*, 7, 163–76.

Lindau, Mona (1984) Phonetic differences in glottalic consonants. *Journal of Phonetics*, 12, 147–55.

Lindau, Mona (1985) The story of /r/. In V. Fromkin (ed.), *Phonetic Linguistics: Essays in honor of Peter Ladefoged*, Orlando, Fla.: Academic Press.

Lindblom, Björn (1990) Explaining phonetic variation: a sketch of the H&H theory. In W. J. Hardcastle and A. Marchal (eds.), *Speech Production and Speech Modeling*, Dordrecht: Kluwer, 403–39.

Lindqvist-Gauffin, J. and Sundberg, J. (1976) Acoustic properties of the nasal tract. *Phonetica*, 33, 161–8.

Lubker, J. (1968) An EMG-cinefluorographic investigation of velar function during normal speech production. *Cleft Palate Journal*, 5, 1.

Lyons, Richard F. (1982) A computational model of filtering, detection and compression in the cochlea. *Proceedings of the IEEE International Conference on Acoustics, Speech and Signal Processing*.

Lyons, Richard F. (1997) *Understanding Digital Signal Processing*, Reading, Mass.: Addison-Wesley.

Maddieson, Ian (1984) *Patterns of Sounds*, Cambridge: Cambridge University Press.

Maeda, Shinji (1993) Acoustics of vowel nasalization and articulatory shifts in French nasal vowels. In Marie K. Huffman and Rena A. Krakow (eds.), *Phonetics and Phonology*, vol. 5: *Nasals, nasalization, and the velum*, New York: Academic Press, 147–67.

Markel, J. D. and Gray, A. H., Jr. (1976) *Linear Prediction of Speech*, New York: Springer-Verlag.

Marple, L. (1987) *Digital Spectral Analysis with Applications*, Englewood Cliffs, NJ: Prentice-Hall.

McDonough, Joyce (1993) The phonological representation of laterals. *UCLA Working Papers in Phonetics*, 83, 19–32.

McDonough, Joyce and Ladefoged, Peter (1993) Navajo stops. *UCLA Working Papers in Phonetics*, 84, 151–64.

McGurk, H. and MacDonald, J. (1976) Hearing lips and seeing voices. *Nature*, 264, 746–8.

Miller, George A. and Nicely, Patricia E. (1955) An analysis of perceptual confusions among some English consonants. *Journal of the Acoustical Society of America*, 27, 338–52.

Miller, J. D. (1989) Auditory-perceptual interpretation of the vowel. *Journal of the Acoustical Society of America*, 85, 2114–34.

Moll, K. L. (1962) Velopharyngeal closure in vowels. *Journal of Speech and Hearing Research*, 5, 30–7.

Moore, B. C. J. (1982) *An Introduction to the Psychology of Hearing*, 2nd edn., New York: Academic Press.

Moore, B. C. J. and Glasberg, B. R. (1983) Suggested formulae for calculating auditory-filter bandwidths and excitation patterns. *Journal of the Acoustical Society of America*, 74, 750–3.

Mrayati, M., Carré, R., and Guérin, B. (1988) Distinctive regions and modes: a new theory of speech production. *Speech Communication*, 7, 257–86.

O'Shaughnessy, Douglas (1987) *Speech Communication: Human and machine*, Reading, Mass.: Addison-Wesley.

Parzen, E. (1962) On estimation of a probability density function and mode. *Annals of Mathematical Statistics*, 33, 1065–76.

Patterson, R. D. (1976) Auditory filter shapes derived from noise stimuli. *Journal of the Acoustical Society of America*, 59, 640–54.

Perkell, J. (1971) Physiology of speech production: a preliminary study of two suggested revisions of the features specifying vowels. *Quarterly Progress Report*, 102, 123–39. Research Institute of Electronics, MIT.

Petursson, M. (1973) Quelques remarques sur l'aspect articulatoire et acoustique des constrictives intrabuccales Islandaises. *Travaux l'Institut de Phonetique de Strasbourg*, 5, 79–99.

Pickles, J. O. (1988) *An Introduction to the Physiology of Hearing*, 2nd edn., New York: Academic Press.

Potter, Ralph K., Kopp, George A., and Green, Harriet (1947) *Visible Speech*, Dordrecht: Van Nostrand.

Qi, Yingyong (1989) Acoustic features of nasal consonants. Unpublished Ph.D. diss., Ohio State University.

Raphael, L. J. and Bell-Berti, F. (1975) Tongue musculature and the feature of tension in English vowels. *Phonetica*, 32, 61–73.

Rayleigh, J. W. S. (1896) *The Theory of Sound*, London: Macmillan; repr. 1945, New York: Dover.

Repp, Bruno (1986) Perception of the [m]–[n] distinction in CV syllables. *Journal of the Acoustical Society of America*, 79, 1987–99.

Rosenblum, L. D., Schmuckler, M. A., and Johnson, J. A. (1997) The McGurk effect in infants. *Perception & Psychophysics*, 59, 347–57.

Schroeder, M. R., Atal, B. S., and Hall, J. L. (1979) Objective measure of certain speech signal degradations based on masking properties of human auditory perception. In B. Lindblom and S. Öhman (eds.), *Frontiers of Speech Communication Research*, London: Academic Press.

Sekiyama, K. and Tohkura, Y. (1993) Inter-language differences in the influence of visual cues in speech perception. *Journal of Phonetics*, 21, 427–44.

Seneff, Stephanie (1988) A joint synchrony/mean-rate model of auditory speech processing. *Journal of Phonetics*, 16, 55–76.

Shadle, C. (1985) The acoustics of fricative consonants. *RLE Technical Report*, 506, MIT.

Shadle, C. (1991) The effect of geometry on source mechanisms of fricative consonants. *Journal of Phonetics*, 19, 409–24.

Shannon, C. E. and Weaver, W. (1949) *The Mathematical Theory of Communication*. Urbana: University of Illinois.

Shepard, R. N. (1972) Psychological representation of speech sounds. In E. E. David and P. B. Denes (eds.) *Human Communication: A unified view*. New York: McGraw-Hill, 67–113.

Shepard, R. N., Kilpatric, D. W., and Cunningham, J. P. (1975) The internal representation of numbers. *Cognitive Psychology*, 7, 82–138.

Slaney, M. (1988) Lyons' cochlear model. *Apple Technical Report*, 13. Apple Corporate Library, Cupertino, Calif.

Stevens, K. N. (1972) The quantal nature of speech: evidence from articulatory-acoustic data. In E. E. David, Jr. and P. B. Denes (eds.), *Human Communication: a unified view*, New York: McGraw-Hill, 51–66.

Stevens, K. N. (1987) Interaction between acoustic sources and vocal-tract configurations for consonants. In *Proceedings of the Eleventh International Conference on Phonetic Sciences*, Tallin, vol. 3, pp. 385–9.

Stevens, K. N. (1989) On the quantal nature of speech. *Journal of Phonetics*, 17, 3–45.

Stevens, K. N. and House, A. S. (1955) Development of a quantitative description of vowel articulation. *Journal of the Acoustical Society of America*, 27, 484–93.

Stevens, S. S. (1957) Concerning the form of the loudness function. *Journal of the Acoustical Society of America*, 29, 603.

Stockwell, R. P. (1973) Problems in the interpretation of the great English vowel shift. In M. E. Smith (ed.), *Studies in Linguistics in Honor of George L. Trager*, The Hague: Mouton, 344–62.

Stone, M. (1991) Toward a model of three-dimensional tongue movement. *Journal of Phonetics*, 19, 309–20.

Straka, Georges (1965) *Album phonetique*, Laval: Les Presses de l'Université Laval.

Syrdal, A. K. and Gophal, H. S. (1986) A perceptual model of vowel recognition based on the auditory representation of American English vowels. *Journal of the Acoustical Society of America*, 79, 1086–1100.

Terbeek, D. (1977) A cross-language multidimensional scaling study of vowel perception. *UCLA Working Papers in Phonetics*, 37, 1–271.

Traunmüller, H. (1981) Perceptual dimension of openness in vowels. *Journal of the Acoustical Society of America*, 69, 1465–75.

Walker, S., Bruce, V. and O'Malley, C. (1995) Facial identity and facial speech processing: Familiar faces and voices in the McGurk effect. *Perception & Psychophysics*, 57, 1124–33.

Wright, James T. (1986) The behavior of nasalized vowels in the perceptual vowel space. In J. J. Ohala and J. J. Jaeger (eds.), *Experimental Phonology*, New York: Academic Press, 45–67.

Zwicker, E. (1961) Subdivision of the audible frequency range into critical bands (*Frequenzgruppen*). *Journal of the Acoustical Society of America*, 33, 248.

Zwicker, E. (1975) Scaling. In Wolf D. Keidel and William D. Neff (eds.), *Auditory System: Physiology (CNS), behavioral studies, psychoacoustics*, Berlin: Springer-Verlag.

Answers to Selected Short-answer Questions

Chapter 1   Basic acoustics and acoustic filters

2.   1,000 ms = 1 sec
    200 ms = 0.2 sec
     10 ms = 0.01 sec
 1,210 ms = 1.21 sec

7.   The pass bands and reject bands of this double pass filter are shown below (see figure A1).

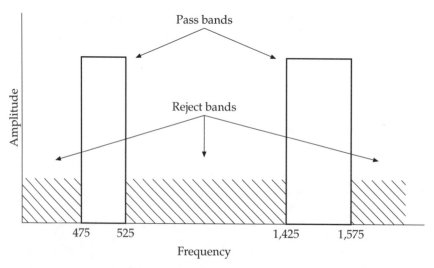

Figure A1   Pass bands and reject bands of the filter described in question 1.7.

Chapter 2 Digital signal processing

2. Nyquist frequencies are:

   8,000 Hz, 5501.25 Hz, 10 Hz

5. Because the ideal lag duration in autocorrelation pitch tracking is the real pitch period of signal (which is what we are doing in pitch tracking) the best lag durations are $1/F_0$.

   $1/100 = 0.01$ sec, $1/200 = 0.005$ sec, $1/204 = 0.0049$ sec

8. The window is: 512/22,000 (0.02327) seconds. Actually, the terms "22 k" or "22 kHz" sampling almost always refer to a 22,050 Hz sampling rate – which would alter these answers a bit.

9. 22,000 samples per second multiplied by 0.02 seconds equals 440 samples.

Chapter 3 Basic audition

1. Six sones = 185,185 µPa. Subjectively double is 12 sones which equals 758,928 µPa. This sound, which is subjectively twice as loud, has a sound pressure level that is four times greater.

3. 7 kHz = 22   Bark   1 kHz = 8.5 Bark
    8 kHz = 22.5 Bark   2 kHz = 13   Bark
    ───────────────   ─────────────────
              0.5 Bark   4.5 Bark

Chapter 4 Speech perception

3. With the submatrix for [d] and [ð]

	d	ð
d	0.727	0
ð	0.015	0.515

   we can calculate similarity (s),

   $$S_{dð} = \frac{0.0 + 0.015}{0.727 + 0.515} = 0.0124$$

   and then distance (d),

   $$\begin{aligned} d_{dð} &= -\ln(S_{dð}) \\ &= -\ln(0.0124) \\ &= 4.39 \end{aligned}$$

which is greater than the distance between [s] and [ð].

$$d_{zð} = -\ln(S_{zð})$$
$$= -\ln(0.081)$$
$$= 2.51$$

5. The data on how auditory and visual perceptual spaces combine to let us predict the audio/visual McGurk effect are clearly compatible with the view that listeners perceive speech gestures – conveyed by both audition and vision. Of course, "compatibility" doesn't equal proof, but scientists do tend to accept the theory that is compatible with the widest range of available data.

Chapter 5   The acoustic theory of speech production

1. Amplitude at 1 kHz = −38 dB
   2 kHz = −41 dB
                   −3 dB

   The spectrum seems to be tilted so that the amplitude goes down by 3 dB over this frequency inteval.

3. Using formula: $F_n = \dfrac{(2n-1)c}{4L}$

Table A1   Formant frequencies in (Hz) of vocal tracts of 12, 15, and 18

	n	$(2n-1)c$	$L = 12$	15	18
F_1	1	35,000	729	583	486
F_2	2	105,000	2,188	1,750	1,458
F_3	3	175,000	3,646	2,917	24,331

Chapter 6   Vowels

2. Using formula: $f = \dfrac{c}{2\pi}\sqrt{\dfrac{A_c}{A_b l_b l_c}}$ with $A_b = 3$, $l_b = 4$, and $l_c = 2$.

   We have $A_b l_b l_c = 24$ and $\dfrac{c}{2\pi} = 5{,}570.4$. Thus, for values of A_c between 0.05 and 2 we have:

A_c	0.05	0.1	0.15	0.2
F_1	254	360	440	509

   When A_c equals 0, F_1 also equals 0.

6. For the mid and low vowels in Mazatec we can see a peak for the second harmonic between the F_0 (first harmonic) and F_1 peaks. Unlike the LPC spectra

in figure 6.10a in which the lowest peak is always the F_1, in the auditory spectra of figure 6.10b the lowest vocal tract resonance (F_1) may be the second or third peak in the spectrum. With a high pitched voice we might even find that F_0 and F_1 form a single peak in the auditory spectrum. So it would seem that if F_1 can be the first, second, or third peak it would be difficult to devise an automatic formant tracker for F_1 in auditory spectra.

Chapter 7   *Fricatives*

2. As the articulators come together at the beginning of a fricative, and as the constriction is released at the end of a fricative, the assumption that the front and back cavities are uncoupled is likely to be wrong. This is because the constriction is less narrow at these times. Thus, at fricative onset and offset we might expect to see spectral peaks at the resonant frequencies of the back cavity.

4. This question is mysterious to some students. Acoustic coupling is the key. When the front and back cavities are strongly coupled (as in vowels) their resonances merge to form stable regions. But when the front and back cavities are not strongly coupled (as in fricatives) the front cavity resonances "skip" the back cavity resonances (figure 7.6). So, if quantal regions define distinctive features, and if as the figures imply quantal regions for fricatives and vowel place of articulation differ, then vowel and fricative place features must be different. This falls under a general observation that acoustic considerations tend to lead us to conclude that vowels and consonants have different features, while articulatory considerations lead us to conclude that vowels and consonants can be described with the same features.

Chapter 8   *Stops and affricates*

2. Figure A2 (see p. 178) is a picture of the formant transitions measured from figure 8.7. The vertical line-up point is the onset of the vowel steady-state for each of the dV syllables in that figure. The heavy lines show the formant transitions and the light lines show these extended back so that they interesect with each other. I chose the locus frequency giving greater weight to the longer, easier to measure transitions of [u] and [i].

4. Yes, affricates do have stop release bursts. Because they have a stop component, it stands to reason that the same pressure build-up and release that we see in nonaffricated stops would also be present in affricates. However, affricate release bursts might be auditorily masked by the sudden onset of frication that occurs soon after stop release.

Chapter 9   *Nasals and laterals*

1. The light damping peak in figure 9.2 has a steeper "skirt". Energy falls off more gradually from the heavy damping peak than from the light damping peak.

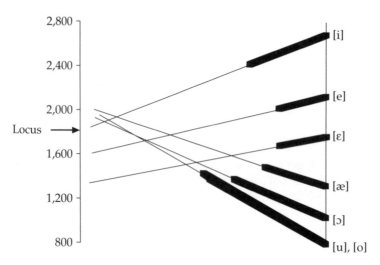

Figure A2 The F_2 locus frequency of /d/.

3. Assume that the mouth cavity is 4 cm long in a palatal nasal. Then the lowest antiformant frequency is:

$$A_1 = \frac{(2 \times 1 + 1)c}{4L}$$

$$= \frac{c}{4L}$$

$$= \frac{35{,}000}{16}$$

$$= 2{,}188$$

5. What breathy vowels and nasalized vowels have in common is that they both have increased energy at low frequencies, as compared with the spectra of nonnasalized modal vowels. The voice spectrum in breathy vowels has a steeper spectral slope, and thus relatively more low frequency energy. In nasalized vowels there are two low frequency resonances (the "nasal" and "oral" first formants) and the antiformants in nasalized vowels attenuate higher frequency energy in the spectrum.

So "spontaneous nasalization" may result from a perceptual confusion in which listeners hearing breathy vowels may falsely think that the speaker is producing a nasalized vowel. If nasalized vowels only occur in the context of a nasal consonant, the listener may then parse the mistakenly identified nasalized vowel as a vowel-nasal sequence comparable to other nasalized vowels in the language.

Index